THE WORLD NEWS PRISM
Changing Media, Clashing Ideologies

D0075369

THE
World News Prism
CHANGING MEDIA, CLASHING IDEOLOGIES

William A. Hachten
WITH THE COLLABORATION OF
HARVA HACHTEN

The Iowa State University Press
AMES, IOWA

TO THE MEMORY OF
My Mother and My Father

William A. Hachten is professor of journalism and mass communication at the University of Wisconsin-Madison. He served as director of its School of Journalism and Mass Communication from 1975 to 1980. His earlier books are *Muffled Drums: The News Media in Africa* (1971) and *The Supreme Court on Freedom of the Press* (1968), both published by the Iowa State University Press, and *Mass Communication in Africa: An Annotated Bibliography* (1971).

© 1981 The Iowa State University Press. All rights reserved

Printed by The Iowa State University Press, Ames, Iowa 50010

First edition, 1981

Library of Congress Cataloging in Publication Data

Hachten, William A.
  The world news prism.

  Bibliography: p.
  Includes index.
  1. Foreign news.   2. Communication, International.
3. Journalism—Political aspects.   I. Hachten, Harva.
II. Title.
PN4784.F6H3   070.4'33   81–2421

ISBN 0–8138–1580–0   AACR2

CONTENTS

PREFACE

THIS OVERVIEW of trends and developments in international news is designed for students in journalism and mass communication who are concerned with how news is gathered and moves about the world. My hope is that their teachers as well as journalists and others will also find it of interest.

Since the end of World War II in 1945, the world has changed greatly and dramatically. Here, I am examining how two of the momentous postwar changes—the technological revolution in communication and information and the emergence of the decolonized, improverished nations of the Third World—have profoundly affected the international news system.

Communications and information systems and technologies are at the leading edge of social, economic, political, and scientific developments in the world today. And particularly with the rise of television as the central mass medium for both entertainment and news, the public has developed a more immediate interest in how news is collected and seeks a fuller understanding of the symbiotic relationship between events and those who report them. It will find, I hope, some insights in the following pages.

In the preparation of this book, several persons were particularly helpful. Two authorities on international communications, Professors Albert Hester and John T. McNelly, provided valuable comments and suggestions on the manuscript. The editor, Elizabeth McClurkin of the Iowa State University Press, made a number of useful improvements. Most helpful was my wife, Harva Hachten, who as my collaborator read the manuscript carefully and rewrote parts of it. I consider myself fortunate to have married a journalist who shares my interest in international communication and knows how to write. Finally, I am indebted to the Research Committee of the Graduate School at the University of Wisconsin-Madison for support of some of the research on this book.

W. A. H.

INTRODUCTION

O<small>N</small> an August day in 1969, an estimated 600 million people watched Neil Armstrong take man's first walk on the moon. They sat in front of their television sets not as Americans, Frenchmen, Africans, or Japanese, but as earthlings watching in awe as one of their kind first stepped onto another planet.

That quintessential media event vividly illustrates the "technetronic" age, the melding of technology and electronics, that planet earth has entered—a new era whose potential we but dimly perceive, whose complicated gadgetry only few of us totally grasp, whose social, political, and economic consequences are accelerating change and cleavages among the nations of the world.

For the world we live in today is changing rapidly, in no small part because worldwide television, communication satellites, high-speed transmission of news and data, and other computer and electronic hardware have transformed the ways that nations and peoples communicate with one another. The fact that a news event can be transmitted almost instantaneously to newsrooms and onto television screens around the world is as important as the event itself. Long-distance mass communication has become a rudimentary central nervous system for our fragile, shrinking, and increasingly interdependent world.

This book describes and analyzes the dramatically altered role of today's transnational news media in the technetronic age.

On the one hand are the technological and operational changes taking place in the international news media, with their new capability for global communication that is reshaping "spaceship earth." On the other hand, and equally important, are the problems these changes have wrought, most notably the conflicts over transnational news gathering and dissemination and the worldwide impact of television programming, motion pictures, radio broadcasting, and other aspects of Western mass culture.

Unquestionably, the current clashes and disputes over international communication between the West, the Socialist nations, and the Third World are serious and disturbing. Such catch phrases as "free flow of information," "media imperialism," and "new world information order" suggest the profound ideological and political differences over the ways the news media should be organized and controlled.

The concern here is with the excitement and anguish of various facets of this change and the effects on transnational journalism and mass communication. This book is intended to provide some insights into how and why international news communication is evolving and where it is headed.

Few of us can appreciate, much less fully understand, the meaning of the information revolution we are living through, a revolution that has enveloped us virtually unnoticed. The major artifacts of this quiet revolution are the computer and the communication satellite—sophisticated electronic devices we rarely see but which have become as much a part of our lives as the electric light. As with other aspects of modern life, journalism and mass communication recently have made quantum leaps in scope and reach.

We may not be aware of how our perceptions of the world are being changed by the transformed news system, but we quickly learn to take that system for granted. If there is another takeover of an American embassy, or outbreak of warfare in the Middle East, or a coup d'etat in Latin America, we expect to see live television reports the same day via satellite. We are interested but not surprised to see detailed, computer-refined pictures of Mars or Jupiter. We do not wonder that we and most of the world can watch the Olympic games on television from half a world away.

In a broader context, the fact that information, including urgent news, can now be communicated almost instantly to almost anywhere has profound implications for international organization and interaction. To grasp fully what is happening all around us, we must modify our ways of looking at the world and our place in it. We need new perceptions of international communication and its potential to shape and direct the world's changes and adjustments during the remaining years of the twentieth century.

Irresistibly, a new global society of sorts is emerging, and the media of mass communication, along with telecommunications and air transportation, are providing the essential linkages that make interaction and cooperation—and frictions—possible. Full understanding of the nature of this new society requires that today's students of international communication be conversant with world affairs and able to recognize significant trends as they occur. Further, they must keep up with technological innovations in communication media and try to assess their impact. (Communication satellites are just one example of the truly revolutionary impact that communication technology has had on the modern world. The role of transistor radios in the Third World is another example. In many ways the modern world is itself a product of our greatly enhanced ability to communicate.) Finally, students of international communication must be attuned to the roles and functions of mass communication in changing the political and social relationships of the world's peoples.

The interplay of these three elements makes the study of international communication fascinating and important. The major emphasis throughout this book is on the journalistic aspects of international communication—the new problems and perils of reporting the news, the important but imperfect and controversial ways that journalists keep the world informed.

The first part of the book concerns the changing media—the ways that international journalism is adapting to altering global conditions and utilizing the new hardware of our information age. Some of the fundamental changes that are bringing all peoples of the world—for better or worse—much closer together are broadly outlined. Today, for the first time in history, all nations, however remote, have stepped onto the stage of the modern world. What happens in Uganda or Indonesia has global meaning and often sends repercussions around the world, in part because events there are reported. But more important, there is a degree of interdependence among all peoples and nations that never existed before. We Americans, perhaps, are much slower than others to recognize this. Since our families, jobs, and local communities are of primary and immediate concern, most people, including our leaders, do not perceive the rapid and fundamental changes taking place, changes directly related to our expanded powers of long-distance communication.

For the world has been evolving an international news system that moves information and mass culture ever faster and in greater volume to any place on earth where an antenna can be put up on a short wave radio. Although politics, economic disparities, cultural differences, and ideology keep us apart on most issues, the international news system has on occasion made us one community if only for a few brief moments—as when Neil Armstrong took that "one giant leap for mankind."

Actually, the reportage of Armstrong's walk has further relevance to this book because the new technetronic age is partly an outgrowth of the exploration of space. The communication satellite, high-speed data transmission, and sophisticated computer technology are by-products of space technology and all are playing integral roles in the revolutions of international communication and transnational journalism.

The modern world's practice of collecting and distributing news around the globe is only about a hundred years old and was initiated by news agencies of the United States and the great imperial powers, Britain and France. Today, the world agencies— the Associated Press and United Press International (U.S.), Reuters (Britain), and Agence France Presse (France)—are still the principal conduits of transnational news, although they and other media have been transformed by the new space-age technology. Change has been coming so quickly that it is often difficult to stay current with the ways news is being moved. And to understand the future potential of these space-age gadgets is like trying to perceive in 1905 what the absurd horseless carriage would do in time to the cities and lifestyles of the twentieth century.

Furthermore, technology is modifying some of the institutions of transnational communication. Subtly and almost imperceptibly, various media, especially the major news agencies, are evolving from national to increasingly international, or better, supranational, institutions of mass communication. The highly successful *International Herald Tribune* is widely used by a sophisticated non-American readership, and *Time* and *Newsweek* publish special editions truly international in outlook. This trend is controversial, but there is no doubt that it is happening as a response to the needs of a shrinking world. Concomitantly, English is evolving into the world's media language. The logic of mass communication requires that sender and receiver understand a common language, and so far, English, the language of science and technology, is it.

The international news media, however, are unevenly distributed among nations, and this has created serious problems between the haves and have-nots in mass communication. Moreover, the explosion of international communication technology has coincided with the post–World War II decolonization of the Third World, and the penetration of Western communications into the independent nations thus created has been perceived by some as a new attempt to reassert the domination of the former colonial powers.

The remainder of this book focuses on the differences that frustrate and at times inhibit the flow of international news and divide journalists and mass communicators: political and ideological differences, economic disparities, geographic and ethnic divisions.

The conflicts and frictions in international communication, seemingly ever sharper and more abrasive, arise from divergent concepts of mass communication. In the concept of the press that has evolved in Western democratic nations, which dominate international news gathering, the journalist and the press are relatively independent of government, free to report directly to the public that uses the information to assess its governors. This view is unacceptable to the Communist nations that, following the teachings of Lenin, have placed their media fully within the governmental structure to better serve the goals of the state. In the numerous, mostly impoverished nations of the Third World (neither Western nor Communist), a similar theory—the Developmental concept—has been emerging, which holds that all mass media, domestic and foreign, must be mobilized to serve the great goals of nation building and economic development.

The clash of these concepts and debates on controls on the flow of news have been reverberating in recent years through international organizations such as United Nations Educational, Scientific and Cultural Organization and international professional media groups such as the International Press Institute and the Inter American Press Association. Although efforts to reconcile these conflicting approaches to mass communication have been painful and slow, an accommodation is necessary to world peace and understanding. Western journalists believe strongly that their ability to gather news abroad is becoming increasingly impaired as more and more Third World and Socialist nations frustrate and block the activities of foreign reporters. Authoritarian governments with controlled press systems resent what they consider the negative reporting of Western media and as a result just keep foreign reporters out. For their part, many non-Western nations resent what they consider to be the domination of the world news flow by a few Western news media. They see a kind of "media imperialism" imposing alien values on developing societies through a one-way flow of news. This monopolistic concentration of the power to communicate, they say, does not serve the aspirations of the many poor nations of the Third World.

The deep differences between the haves and have-nots in world news communication reflect closely other differences between rich and poor nations. And despite the impressive gains in the technical ability to communicate more widely and quickly, the disturbing evidence is that the world may be growing further apart rather than closer together. As with so much else in modern life, technology seems to race far ahead of our political skills to use it for the greatest good of all.

The world's system of distributing news can be likened to a crystal prism. What is considered in one place as the straight white light of truth travels through the prism and is refracted and bent into a variety of colors and shades. One person's truth becomes to another biased reporting or propaganda, depending on where the light strikes the prism and where it emerges. As we understand and accept the optics of a prism for measuring the spectrum of light, so must we understand and accept the transecting planes of different cultural and political traditions that refract divergent perceptions of our world.

At this point, I must acknowledge how the light refracts for me. In considering the problems of international news, I have tried to be sympathetic to the views and frustrations of non-Western nations and the enormous difficulties they face. Journalism is a highly subjective pursuit, tempered and shaped by the political conditions and cultural traditions of the societies where it is practiced; the world and the news do look differently from Moscow, Lagos, or Jakarta than they do from New York or London.

As a product of the Western press tradition, I believe journalists should disagree at times with political leaders and with other journalists and the owners of the media. The essence of journalism is diversity of ideas and the freedom to express them. I find it difficult to disagree with Albert Camus, who wrote that "a free press can of course be good or bad, but certainly without freedom, it will never be anything but bad. . . . Freedom is nothing else but a chance to be better, whereas enslavement is a certainty of the worse."

And in the dangerous, strife-ridden world of the late twentieth century, I believe the billions of people inhabiting this planet deserve to know all the happenings that affect their lives and well-being. Only journalists who are free and independent of authoritarian controls and other constraints can begin the difficult task of reporting the news and information we all need to know.

THE WORLD NEWS PRISM
Changing Media, Clashing Ideologies

1

Communication for an Interdependent World

By every indication the global human society is entering a period of change of historical proportions. Some call it the era of limited resources; some see it as the start of the new world economic order; some call it the communications age, or the post industrial society or the information age; but nearly every discipline and sector of society senses the shifts taking place. By whatever name, . . . we are moving along a trajectory leading to a global human culture in which events across the world affect us with the same speed and impact as if they happened next door.

Congressman George E. Brown
(D-California)

Perhaps one of the most significant photographs of modern times was taken in July 1969 during the Apollo 11 mission to the moon. The astronauts photographed the earthrise as seen from the moon, and there our planet was, like a big, blue, cloudy marble. The widely reprinted picture illuminated the fragility and cosmic insignificance of our spaceship earth.

That stunning photograph coincided with the worldwide concern about ecology and global pollution; even more, it made it easy to grasp why many scientists already treat that cloudy, blue marble as a complete biological system in which change in one part will inevitably affect other parts.

Certainly in the years since, concerned persons around the world have become more aware of our global interdependence. The great historical reality of our times is that the world is becoming a single rudimentary community—with all that that implies. Today's world is faced with urgent and complex problems, most of them interrelated: overpopulation, poverty, famine, depletion of natural (especially energy) resources, pollution of the biosphere, the nuclear threat of the arms buildup, the ever widening gap between the rich and poor nations, and widespread inflation.

Although they may be found in some places and not in others, these problems are truly international, and amelioration, much less solution, of any of them must depend on cooperation and goodwill among nations. And before that, there must be information and understanding of these challenges, for these are crises of interdependence. No one nation or even combination of nations can deal effectively with such global concerns as the oil scarcity, international monetary crises, pollution of the oceans, terrorism and hijacking of jet airliners, or widespread grain shortages. Yet the blinders of nationalism and modern tribalism continue to influence political leaders everywhere to react to international problems with narrow and provincial responses.

Lester Brown, an authority on global needs, has described the problems of the late twentieth century as "unique in their scale." Previous catastrophes—famines, floods, earthquakes, volcanic eruptions—were local and temporary. But now, although the world's more pressing concerns can be solved only through multinational or global cooperation, the institutions to cope with them are largely national. And since each new technology creates additional problems but not the institutions capable of solving them, Brown sees conditions worsening in the years immediately ahead.

"Given the scale and complexity of these problems, the remainder of the twentieth century will at best be a traumatic period for mankind, even with a frontal attack on the principal threats to human well-being," Brown wrote. "At worst it will be catastrophic. At issue is whether we can grasp the nature and dimensions of the emerging threats to our well-being, whether we can create an integrated global economy and a workable world order, and whether we can reorder global priorities so that the quality of life will improve rather than deteriorate."[1]

Brown's view of world problems, shared by people in many countries, is still not understood by any great numbers of them. We Americans, for example, periodically turn inward and become parochial, failing to comprehend how domestic problems have roots in events that occur thousands of miles away. During the 1976 presidential campaign, for instance, pollster George Gallup discovered that only 5 percent of the public felt that the nation's chief problem was foreign policy or defense. Voters cited as the "most important problems facing the nation" the high cost of living, 38 percent; unemployment, 24 percent; and dissatisfaction with government, 13 percent.

But by the end of the decade, the hard realities of the energy crunch and other foreign events subjected the public here (and abroad) to another crash course on global interdependency. Historically, American interest in world events has ebbed and flowed, but events in Southwest Asia as the 1980s began sharply reawakened Americans' interest in foreign affairs. The long ordeal of the kidnapped hostages at the American embassy in Iran and the Russian incursion into Afghanistan altered American public opinion more sharply than any event since Pearl Harbor. But even without these highly emotional and dangerous developments, the very nature of the problems of the late twentieth century—transnational in scope and beyond the ability of this or any single nation to solve by itself—may be changing our traditional provincialism.

Moreover, each new event in the continuing oil crisis—the latest price hikes by OPEC, oil cutoff in Iran, new discoveries in Mexico, political instability and unrest in the Persian Gulf—is rapidly disseminated to a world audience that reacts almost instantly.

The world's political structures, many believe, must be reshaped to enable us to cope with these global challenges. Hence the great importance, despite their serious shortcomings, of international organizations such as the United Nations and its attendant agencies.

Professor Edwin Reischauer, former U.S. ambassador to Japan, feels the response to the problem must start by changing individuals through a profound reshaping of education. Proliferating technology is fast destroying the cushioning that once existed between the different nations and cultures of the world. This in turn rapidly increases not only interdependence, but tensions as well.

"While the world is in the process of becoming a single great mass of humanity—a global community, as it is sometimes called," Reischauer wrote, "the very diverse national and cultural groupings that make up the world's population retain attitudes and habits more appropriate to a different technological age."

In the United States, he declared, education "is not moving rapidly enough in the right directions to produce the knowledge about the outside world and the attitudes toward other peoples that may be essential for human survival within a generation or two. This, I feel, is a much greater international problem than the military balance of power that absorbs so much of our attention today."[2]

The shortcomings of U.S. education that Reischauer criticized were illustrated by a government survey in 1979; it showed that 27 percent of high school seniors believed Golda Meir was president of Egypt, 40 percent thought Israel was an Arab nation, and 17 percent estimated that the U.S. population was greater than that of either China or the Soviet Union. And a 1977 Gallup Poll found that half of all Americans did not know that the United States had to import petroleum to meet its needs.

Few Americans, furthermore, know foreign languages. In 1979, a Presidential Commission on Foreign Language and International Studies concluded that "America's scandalous incompetence in foreign languages . . . explains our dangerously inadequate understanding of world affairs." And the situation is getting worse. In 1965, only one high school student in four studied a foreign language; at the end of the 1970s, the figure was one in seven. In 1966, 34 percent of U.S. colleges required a foreign language for admission; 14 years later, only 8 percent did. The commission warned that American "vital interests are impaired by the fatuous notion that our competence in other languages is irrelevant."[3]

Professor Robert Ward of Stanford University has described the extent of our current neglect of international education at all levels as shocking. He might have added that most American news media pay far too little attention to news from abroad. What worries experts in this field is that ignorance and apathy about the world beyond America's borders may undermine this country's political, diplomatic, and economic influence. The next generation of Americans will be ill-prepared to grapple with global problems.

As important as formal education is, its influence sometimes does not change attitudes or improve understanding until generations have passed. In immediate terms, the flow of information and news throughout the globe will have a greater impact on the world's ability to understand its problems and dangers and somehow respond to them.

Since World War II especially, an intricate and worldwide network of international news media has evolved, providing an expanded capability for information flow. This relationship between the ability and the need to communicate rapidly has resulted from the interaction of two gradual processes: the evolution toward a single global society and the movement of civilization beyond four great bench marks of human communication—speech, writing, printing, electronic communications (telephone and radio)—into a fifth era of long-distance instant communication based on communication satellites and computer technology.

Harold Lasswell believes that the mass media revolution has accelerated the tempo and direction of world history. What would have happened later has happened sooner, and changes in timing may have modified substantive development.[4] Following the nuclear accident at Three Mile Island and the worldwide televised reporting of that event, nations and informed persons everywhere quickly modified their attitudes about nuclear energy. Thirty years earlier, public reactions to such an event would have been much slower and less perceptible.

Zbigniew Brzezinski coined the word "technetronic" to describe this new age in which communications will play a greater international role.

> The post-industrial society is becoming a "technetronic" society: a society that is shaped culturally, psychologically, socially, and economically by the impact of technology and electronics—particularly in the area of computers and communications.

But while our immediate reality is being fragmented, global reality increasingly absorbs the individual, involves him, and even occasionally overwhelms him. Communications are the obvious, immediate cause. . . . The changes wrought by communications and computers make for an extraordinarily interwoven society whose members are in continuous and close audio-visual contact—constantly interacting, instantly sharing the most intense social experiences, and prompted to increased personal involvement in even the most distant problems. . . . By 1985, distance will be no excuse for delayed information from any part of the world to the powerful urban nerve centers that will mark major concentrations of the people on earth.[5]

It seems paradoxical that even with this greatly enhanced capability of involvement in world affairs, comparatively few people are well informed or even care much about what happens beyond their borders. But for those comparative few who do follow public affairs (and they are found in every nation), perceptions of the world are being shaped and organized by this revolution in long-distance instant communications.

Our ability or lack of it to use the fruits of this revolution is directly related to our success or failure to act decisively and in concert as a world community. International experts worry whether the world can organize itself and deal effectively with what UN Secretary General Kurt Waldheim called the six interrelated world problems: mass poverty, population, food, energy, military expenditure, and the world monetary system. Yet to organize, we must communicate, since communication is the neural system of any organization. The extent and ability to communicate determines the boundaries of any community—be it a primitive tribe in Papua, New Guinea, or a global society—and only expanded and more effective communication can make possible a viable global community.

The technology to circulate that information exists, but the barriers of illiteracy, poverty, and political constraints keep too many people in the world from receiving it. The illiteracy situation is particularly discouraging. Even though the proportion of illiterate adults declined from 44.4 to 32 percent between 1950 and 1979, the actual number increased from 700 million to 810 million, according to UNESCO. And most experts believe these figures underestimate the extent of illiteracy. The situation has been aggravated by the establishment since World War II of many new but poverty-stricken nations comprising about 850 million people, the majority of them illiterate. In 62 of the United Nations' 150 plus member countries, the illiteracy rate is more than 50 percent. In 20 countries, more than 90 percent of the adult population are unable to read or write. In many countries, virtually the entire female population is illiterate, thus severely aggravating the inferior status of women.

Literacy is the key skill for modernization, education, and use of mass media. Illiteracy is widespread in Africa (only 7 percent in Ethiopia, for instance, can read) so it is no wonder that there are only 200 daily newspapers in all of Africa compared with more than 1,770 in the United States. In any country, therefore, the proportion of people able to receive news and information will vary greatly according to the availability of mass media and the ability of people to use the media. Those living in such "information societies" as Japan or the United States are overwhelmed with information and news, while throughout the vast Third World only a tiny fraction of persons are able to participate in the international news flow.

Regardless of where they live, however, too few people take advantage of opportunities to acquire and use information in the solution of urgent transnational problems. The peoples of the dozen or so nations living on the shores of the Mediterranean Sea, for example, are confronted with accelerating pollution that is strangling that body of water. Without an unimpeded flow of information across borders to concerned leaders and experts from Greece to Algeria, corrective action to save the Mediterreanean is impossible; only concerted international cooperation by all nations on the sea's borders can make effective response possible. Fortunately, such an effort has begun.

However, whether the problem is pollution of the seas or proliferation of nuclear weapons, the fact remains that international society is marked by the absence of collective procedures, by competition rather than cooperation, and by the lack of a commitment to a common goal. In other words, anarchy. The world is ruled by nation states, not by an effective international organization, and each state will act according to its own interests and needs.

Political scientist Robert Tucker of Johns Hopkins reminds us that

the prospects for an emergent global community cannot appear promising today. Instead of a universal conscience in the making, throughout most of the world we can observe discrete national consciences in the making. The vision of shared community that, once internalized, could prompt people to sacrifice on behalf of a common good remains at best embryonic. For the time being, the global challenges posed by nuclear weapons, grinding poverty, and burgeoning populations—to mention only the most pressing—will have to be dealt with by a world that is, in many respects, as divided as ever.[6]

While the pessimistic realism of Professor Tucker cannot be denied, there is encouragement to be had in the futuristic views of science writer Arthur C. Clarke regarding the communication satellite:

What we are now doing—whether we like it or not—indeed, whether we wish it or not—is laying the foundation of the first global society. Whether the final planetary authority will be an analogue of the federal systems now existing in the United States or the USSR I do not know. I suspect that, without any deliberate planning, such organizations as the world meteorological and earth resources satellite system and the world communications satellite system (of which INTELSAT is the precursor) will eventually transcend their individual components. At some time during the next century they will discover, to their great surprise, that they are really running the world.

There are many who will regard these possibilities with alarm or distaste, and may even attempt to prevent their fulfillment. I would remind them of the story of the wise English king, Canute, who had his throne set upon the seashore so he could demonstrate to his foolish courtiers that even the king could not command the incoming tide.

The wave of the future is now rising before us. Gentlemen, do not attempt to hold it back. Wisdom lies in recognizing the inevitable—and cooperating with it. In the world that is coming, the great powers are not great enough.[7]

The signs of the inevitable are already visible; a slow but perceptible trend toward internationalization of the world's news media is taking place. The world's news agencies, a few newspapers and magazines, and some aspects of broadcasting are transcending the national states from which they arose. Such a trend will be welcomed by some as a contribution to better world understanding or resented by others as efforts by the West to impose its models on everyone.

The technological capability for worldwide communication has never been greater, but then never have truly global problems and challenges been more urgent and ominous. Too few people anywhere understand these problems or are in a position to cooperate with others in resolving them.

Serious questions can be posed about the adequacy of today's system of global news communication, but there is no doubt about the importance to the world of the newspapers, news agencies, and broadcasters that report the world's news to itself.

Notes

1. Lester R. Brown, *World without Borders* (New York: Vintage Books, 1973), pp. 10-12.
2. Edwin Reischauer, *Toward the 21st Century: Education for a Changing World* (New York: Alfred A. Knopf, 1973), pp. 3-4.
3. *Capital Times* (Madison, Wis.), November 8, 1979, p. 12.
4. Harold D. Lasswell, "The Future of World Communication: Quality and Style of Life," Papers of the East-West Communication Institute, Honolulu, No. 4, (September 1972), p. 3.
5. Zbigniew Brzezinski, *Between Two Ages: America's Role in the Technetronic Era* (New York: Viking Press, 1970), pp. 9-14.
6. Robert W. Tucker, "World Unity: A Goal Still beyond Reach," *Milwaukee Journal*, March 6, 1977, Accent section, p. 9.
7. Arthur C. Clarke, "Beyond Babel: The Century of the Communications Satellite," in *The Process and Effects of Mass Communication*, eds. W. Schramm and D. Roberts (Urbana: University of Illinois Press, 1971), p. 963.

2

International News System

> WHAT we are building now is the nervous
> system of mankind, which will link together
> the whole human race, for better or worse, in a
> unity which no earlier age could have
> imagined.
>
> —ARTHUR C. CLARKE

IN March 1979, a volatile mix of equipment and human failure at Three Mile Island, Pennsylvania, came close to exploding into a major nuclear energy disaster. Day after day, television, radio, and newspapers worldwide chronicled each development in the potential radioactive meltdown crisis, coverage that immediately altered public and governmental attitudes and perceptions in other nations about the desirability of further development of nuclear reactors.

The dramatic significance of this event was enormous. The newspaper space and global air time devoted to the stories of efforts by the experts to cool down the reactor and get the situation under control reflected both the story's importance and the public's expectation to be kept informed. Equally significant but unapparent was the fact that the reportage of an event on a small strip of land in the Susquehanna River in the United States was being conveyed around the globe in a matter of seconds. No one looked upon that fact as anything out of the ordinary. News—like electricity, water, and gas—has become an essential service that is taken for granted. By merely turning on a radio or television set or picking up a newspaper at the door, we expect to find the latest news, whether it be from the Middle East, Europe, Africa, or Three Mile Island.

Indeed, it is hard to remember when breaking news was not available immediately (like any other public utility) at the flick of a switch; the mechanics of its delivery are of little public concern and at best only dimly understood. The fact is, however, that global news communication is of very recent origin. The far-flung apparatus or "system" through which news flows around the world has evolved and developed mainly since World War II along with our modern technetronic society. We learned, for example, of the important events of World War II many hours or even several days after the events—and then through radio or newspapers; just 30 years later, the day's clashes in Vietnam were brought to us in full color on our home television screen at dinner time. It goes without saying that the public's perceptions of a war have always been colored by the way journalists have reported them, but color television pictures of Vietnam had an unusually strong impact on public attitudes.

In modern times, and particularly since 1945, an intricate web of international communication has been spun about the planet, greatly expanding the capability for news and political interaction at a time when the need for information has become so much more urgent. This rapid growth of what Colin Cherry has termed an "explosion" in mass communication around the world has had widespread significance—for world journalism, for the flow of news and information, for the cultural impact of motion pictures and television from the West (sometimes called "cultural imperialism"), and for the institutions of international communication: news agencies; broadcast networks; and international newspapers, magazines, and other publications. As we become an ever more interdependent world community with common problems, if not common goals, the world's ability to communicate effectively to all its parts has been greatly expanded.

As Cherry described it, this communication explosion has three aspects: *geographically*, vast areas of the Southern Hemisphere (Africa, South Asia, Latin America) have been drawn into the communication network for the first time; the *amount* of traf-

fic and the *number* of messages carried in the system have mul-
tiplied geometrically; and the *technical complexity* of both
the new hardware and the skills and specializations to maintain
and run the network have become increasingly sophisticated.

"For two thousand years and more the means of distant communications were various postal services, derived from the
Roman *cursus publicus,* working at the speed of the horse; and
then the explosion hit us, not immediately upon the invention of
the telegraph, but nearly a century later," Cherry wrote. "It is
the sheer suddenness of the explosion which is of such profound
social importance, principally following the Second World War."[1]

From crystal sets in 1920 to a television service in 1937,
Cherry pointed out, was only 17 years. The first transistor appeared in 1948, the first Sputnik followed only 9 years later, and
electronic memory chips, the silicon brains of microcomputers,
came soon after that.

International News System

This expanded international news system is largely an outgrowth of Western news media, especially those of Britain, America, and France. A world news system exists today because the
peoples of the Western democracies wanted and needed world
news, and the great independent newspapers and news agencies,
and later broadcast organizations, have cooperated and competed
to satisfy those wants and needs. Editors and correspondents,
working for independent (that is to say, nongovernmental) news
organizations, have developed the traditions and patterns of providing the almost instantaneous world news upon which people
everywhere have come to rely. The credibility and legitimacy that
such news generally enjoys rests on its usually unofficial and independently gathered nature. The ethic of Western journalism
was summed up over 100 years ago by an editor of the *Times* of
London:

> The first duty of the press is to obtain the earliest and most correct
> intelligence of the events of the time, and instantly, by disclosing them,
> to make them the common property of the nation. The duty of the jour-
> nalist is to present to his readers not such things as statecraft would
> wish them to know but the truth as near as he can attain it.

That nineteenth-century statement represents an ideal; actual practice is often much different. Some transnational media have close, compromising ties to their governments, and all independent media are subject to varying kinds of controls from the corporate interests that own them. Nonetheless, the news media of a handful of Western nations have more freedom and independence to report world news than those of other nations.

Some newspaper and broadcasting organizations report foreign news themselves, but the global workhorses and the linchpins of the world news system are the global news services—Associated Press, United Press International, Reuters, Agence France Presse, and TASS, and it is no coincidence that they come from the United States, Britain, France, and the Soviet Union. In a general sense, the great powers are the great news powers. Today, however, the continued influence of France and Britain in world news is due more to their imperial past than their geopolitical present.

What makes these five organizations world agencies is their ability to report news from almost anywhere to almost anywhere else. (News organizations in two other economic powers—Deutsche Presse Agentur in West Germany and Kyodo News Service in Japan—approach world agency status.) Although they are perceived as dominating world news flow, the four Western agencies are definitely not in a class with powerful multinational corporations such as Exxon or ITT. UPI has been in a shaky financial condition for years, and Scripps Howard annually covers its losses, which run into the millions. AFP receives a reported $65 million a year in subsidies from the French government. Reuters' regular news service is not profitable, although its financial services, which account for 82 percent of its revenue, are. Only AP, which primarily serves 1,298 U.S. newspapers and 5,614 broadcasters, is financially sound. Yet AP's 1980 budget of about $140 million is small potatoes indeed compared to the scope of the giant oil companies such as Exxon, which reported $4 billion in profits for 1979.

An essential support in the world news system is provided by the estimated 120 regional and national news agencies that have emerged since World War II, especially in the Third World. UNESCO reports that national agencies in 90 sovereign countries provide their nations' newspapers and radio and television stations with domestic and foreign news: in 50 countries, the state directly controls or operates these agencies; in the 40 others, one or more of the organizations are cooperatively financed and operated by newspapers or public corporations. The quality and professionalism of these agencies differ greatly. Many are merely government information offices. Most subscribe to or have exchange agreements with one or more of the five world agencies and are the only channels within their countries to receive foreign news from the world agencies, which, in turn, distribute their domestic news abroad. Thus, by exchanging their news with world services, the small national agencies help extend the reach of the world news system.[2]

The dominant and largest institution in the world news system is AP, a cooperative owned by the news media of America. Reuters, AFP, and UPI compete with AP, often very effectively in certain areas such as Africa, but cannot match its comprehensiveness and financial resources. Because it is part of the Soviet government structure, TASS is a special case among world agencies.

Some of the great newspapers of the world—*Times, Daily Telegraph,* and *The Guardian* of London; *Le Monde* of France; *Frankfurter Algemeine* of Germany; *Neue Zürcher Zeitung* of Switzerland; *Asahi* of Japan; *New York Times, Washington Post, Los Angeles Times,* and others of the United States—maintain correspondents abroad, as do the great broadcasting systems—BBC, CBS, NBC, etc.—as well as the news magazines—*Time, Newsweek, L'Express, Der Spiegel,* etc.

However, AP's central role is undisputed. By the agency's count, more than a billion people have daily access to AP news. Like other world agencies, AP uses an extensive network of leased satellite circuits, submarine cables, and radio transmissions to supply newspapers and broadcasters with up-to-the-minute information on developments around the world 24 hours a day. As a result, newspapers and broadcasters in Singapore, Buenos Aires, Johannesburg, or New Delhi can publish or air news bulletins simultaneously, regardless of how distant the news being reported. Three key centers—New York, London, and Tokyo—channel the millions of words and pictures transmitted daily to more than 10,000 subscribers in 110 countries. Without its full and free access to the news and photos of all members of the cooperative, AP would have to spend much more than the $122 million each year in news gathering (still far more than any competitor).

It has been said with some but not much exaggeration that the American's right to know is the world's right to know. For any news story that gets into the American news media can and does flow rapidly around the world and can appear in local media anywhere if it gets by the various gatekeepers that select and reject the news of the day. So hostages in Teheran, revelations about Watergate, a hijacking of an airliner in the Middle East, or a nuclear accident at Three Mile Island (or any other report prepared for the U.S. news media) can and often must be read or viewed or listened to in Africa, Asia, or Latin America. The same, of course, can be said for a story printed first in London, Paris, or Bonn.

The domination of international news by AP and other Western news media is resented by Third World and Socialist nations. Third World nations particularly are dependent on the Western agencies and media to find out about themselves and their neighbors, and they criticize bitterly what they consider a one-way flow from North to South, from the rich to the poor.

Without question, there is a basis to some complaints against the Western media; moreover, far ranging and technically sophisticated as it is, the world's present news system is not as pervasive and efficient as it might be, considering the world's diversity and its need for information. Western journalists do a very imperfect job, and most operate under a variety of constraints, which are discussed in Chapter 6. But it is the only operational system the world has, as Martin Woollacott, *The Guardian*'s chief correspondent in Asia, has pointed out:

For all its defects, the Western foreign press corps is all that the world has got in the way of an efficient international news gathering organization. Even in Western terms, it is a curiously unrepresentative affair, dominated as it is by the big American and British news agencies, newspapers, magazines, and broadcasting organizations. The French are in it, but are a poor second. After them trail the other West European countries, with the Japanese foreign press, in spite of the manpower it deploys, on the periphery. This organization, whose oddities are a product of history, is, however, the only existing means of maintaining a flow of reasonably reliable information between countries. The news establishments of the Communist countries hardly offer a feasible alternative. And the occasional efforts of Asian and African countries to set up their own systems of international news gathering have all been failures. Their papers cannot afford foreign correspondents, and the few projects for Asian and African news agencies have collapsed for lack of money, expertise, and customers.[3]

History of News Distribution

The history of today's international system of news distribution is essentially the story of the world news agencies and their utilization of progressive technological innovations. As the telegraph, cable, teletype, wireless (later radio), and communication satellites became operational, the news agencies or "wire services" (as they were once called) employed each new device to transmit news ever more quickly from capital to capital.

Modern transnational information exchange probably had its beginnings with manuscript newsletters containing political and economic information that were circulated in the late Middle Ages between the various branches of large trading companies. The sixteenth-century newsletters of the house of the Fuggers of Augsburg, Germany, were particularly well known and were read by selected outsiders involved in trade, shipping, or commerce. The contemporary news agencies, however, evolved in nineteenth-century Europe and America. In 1835, Charles Havas, a young Frenchman of Portuguese birth, organized a service with correspondents around Europe to collect news of interest to businessmen, financiers, and diplomats. Employing semaphore signals and carrier pigeons, Havas got the news to his clients more rapidly than the usual post or special courier. Several years later, newspapers began taking advantage of the faster Havas service.

Competitors soon followed. In 1848, Bernard Wolff, a former Havas man, set up a joint news service between German and northern European papers; this later became the Wolff News Agency. Still another former Havas employee, Paul Julius Reuter, a German, established a pigeon post system to deliver the final stock prices between Brussels and Aachen, then the only gap in a telegraph system uniting the commercial centers of Berlin and Paris. After the completed telegraph link rendered this pigeon communication system obsolete, Reuter recognized that he had to be at one terminus of a cable or telegraph to survive. Since the Germans already controlled one end and the French the other, Reuter moved to London; when the cross-channel cable link reached the British capital in 1851, he was there to exploit it. (Reuter's Telegraph Company became known as Reuters.)

Reuters' slogan directive to "follow the cable" (which was the practice of other news agencies as well) epitomized the utilization of the world's increasing capacity in telecommunications. Reuters grew up with and survived the British Empire. Today, it grosses $50 million annually, employs 1,000 full- or part-time correspondents, and sends hundreds of thousands of words daily to clients in 155 countries and territories.

Agence Havas became the dominant news service outside the British Empire—in France, Switzerland, Italy, Spain, Portugal, Egypt (with Reuters), and Central and South America. Following the fall of France in 1940, Agence Havas was dissolved. It was reborn in 1944 as Agence France Presse but required subsidies from the French government to survive financially. In 1957, AFP became autonomous under a controlling board that includes eight directors from French newspapers, although its ties with the French government have remained close.

The three nineteenth-century European services were all profit-making organizations, selling their news to any newspaper willing to buy. American newspapers, finding foreign news expensive to collect, decided to cooperate rather than compete. In 1848, the leading New York papers formed the New York Associated Press to share the costs of obtaining foreign news transmitted on the newly perfected telegraph from Boston. During the remainder of the century, other regional cooperatives were formed (and some dissolved) until 1900, when the system was reorganized and incorporated in New York as the Associated Press.

Because AP members denied the service to competing papers, rival agencies were established. In 1907, E. W. Scripps organized the United Press Association to compete with AP, and William Randolph Hearst formed International News Service in 1909 to supply his own newspapers. UP bought out INS in 1958, and at the end of the 1970s United Press International had 6,972 subscribers worldwide and spent about $78 million annually to collect the news it sold.

However, UPI's revenues were not sufficient to cover the cost of running its worldwide network of 850 journalists in 101 domestic and 65 overseas bureaus. Together they produced eight million words a day for UPI's various state, national, and international wires. The agency's precarious financial situation was a subject of some concern, since most media organizations at least give lip service to the importance of two competing U.S. news agencies here and abroad. The *Wall Street Journal* reported that UPI was losing newspaper clients and had lost millions of dollars since 1961, its most recent profitable year.[4] In September 1979, Scripps Howard announced a $5 million loss for 1978 and in effect put UPI up for sale by offering 45 limited partnerships to a select group of U.S. newspaper and broadcast groups.[5] The prospectus for the offering reported a loss of $20 million between 1974 and 1978.[6]

Atypical among the big five global agencies is TASS, an integral part of the Soviet Union's government. Established in 1918 under the name ROSTA, TASS actively supports official Soviet policies but operates on a worldwide basis, often supplying its service at little or no cost in some countries. Few papers outside the Communist orbit rely on it completely. TASS does provide useful and important information, however, and it has exchange agreements with Western agencies.

These five agencies flowered because of an extensive root system of telegraph and submarine cables. Reuters' early dominance grew out of its accessibility to the cables linking the British Empire. The cable press rate was established at about a penny a word between points in the empire, and this markedly affected what news flowed where around the world. Wireless and shortwave radio started to weaken the importance of the cable, a process that was completed with the development of the INTELSAT communication satellite system, which delivers the news anywhere in the world. The catch phrase of "follow the cable" was replaced by "feed the bird," a reference to the Early Bird communication satellite launched in 1965 and used to relay television news film across the Atlantic.

News, whether by communication satellite or carrier pigeon, is highly perishable, and if interest in a particular story is strong enough, it moves at incredible speed around the world, providing there are no political or technological barriers to its transmission and reception. And it is the communication satellites (comsats) that have made the same-day reporting of international events on the evening television news show commonplace. Live feeds from another continent are easily identifiable as the work of the network involved, but the source of news on film is not as apparent. Most viewers are unaware that much of the foreign news on television is supplied by two television news agencies dominated by American and British interests.

Visnews, the biggest and best known, is the world's leading supplier of international news actuality material for television, servicing more than 170 broadcasters in almost every country that has television. Its promotional boast that Visnews reaches 99 percent of television receivers is largely true.[7] Three-quarters of Visnews shares are owned equally by Reuters and the British Broadcasting Corporation and the remaining one-quarter by public television services of Australia, Canada, and New Zealand. UPITN, the other major film agency, is an enterprise of UPI and Britain's Independent Television News organization.

Through UPI and Reuters, UPITN and Visnews have access to a ready international news network and a huge basic news supply. Visnews supplies BBC news film to the American NBC network, and it sells to the world NBC news film as well as actualities shot by BBC and the Japanese NHK. The other two American networks, CBS and ABC, and the West German DPA-Etes organization also sell their domestic television news abroad.[8]

New Dimensions of International News

The international information system is rapidly moving toward that theoretical condition where it is possible to send information everywhere almost instantly.

With the greatly enhanced technological reach of international communication, the location of a sender or receiver is no longer as important as it once was. The key gatekeepers of world news are still concentrated in New York, London, Paris, and similar metropolitan centers, but it is not necessary to be in those cities to follow the news of the world. A powerful shortwave radio can keep a person almost anywhere in touch with the day's principal events. Furthermore, distance has become increasingly less a factor in the cost of long-distance communication, whether it be private telephone, color television, or news reports bounced off satellites. Essentially the same technological process (and at the same cost) is required to send a news flash via satellite from London to Paris as from London to New York. And the greater the use of the system, the less is the unit cost of messages sent. International communication is tied to computer technology, and in that explosive field the costs of computers are dropping as rapidly as their efficiency is increasing. In addition, the capacity of communication satellites to carry information is expanding.

But the implications of this greatly enhanced capability to communicate rapidly over long distances go beyond the technology and costs. Not only has there been increased speed and volume with greater geographical dispersion of international news flow, but the nature and effects of the content have changed and diversified as well. Instead of mere words and numbers, live television coverage is now delivered to the world's news public, greatly increasing the impact of the audience. As a result, there is a new and significant kind of participation in world news events. The propaganda truism that the report of the event is as important as the event itself has greater impact than ever in the age of media events.

The fact that 600 million people around the world watched on television as Neil Armstrong stepped onto the moon may be perhaps just as important as the moon walk itself, for in those moments, the world was unified and shared a historic experience that transcended political ideology and nationality.

International television coverage of a news event can affect the political impact of the event itself. Millions in Europe in August 1968 watched live television coverage of Soviet tanks invading Czechoslovakia via a relay from Prague to Vienna and thence to the Eurovision network. Consequently, the Soviet Union was never able to convince the world that the invasion was anything other than a ruthless repression of the Dubček regime. Similarly, full television coverage of Arab terrorists holding Israeli athletes hostage at the 1972 Olympic Games in Munich had an impact on the world far greater than merely printed coverage of the tragedy could have had.

Political leaders everywhere have found that global television coverage often adds unwelcome dimension to an event. Polish Communist authorities tried to play down Pope John Paul II's eight-day visit to his native country in June 1979. But worldwide television reportage of the millions of devote Catholics who paid homage to the pontiff lifted the spirits of people everywhere and made the event one of considerable political and religious importance.

Similarly, the television coverage of Olympic Games moves that event beyond the sporting and into the political arena. The worldwide television audience of recent Olympics was estimated to be two billion.

Even the delicate art of diplomacy has been invaded by television cameras and comsats. In November 1977, American television news personalities were participants in the events that eventually led to an Egyptian-Israeli peace treaty, thereby giving birth to the term "media diplomacy." Walter Cronkite of CBS and Barbara Walters of ABC were the conduits for the messages that passed between Egyptian President Anwar Sadat and Israeli Prime Minister Menachem Begin, which culminated in Sadat's visit to Israel to address the Knesset. Thus television served as intermediary between two countries that did not have diplomatic relations. The most dramatic impact was achieved on CBS. Walter Cronkite taped separate interviews with Begin and Sadat, conducted hours apart by telephone in two-way satellite transmissions, but the broadcast of the two interviews, edited and spliced together, gave the effect of a face-to-face encounter between the two leaders, with Cronkite as the go-between. Rightly or wrongly, millions of viewers gained the impression that "Uncle Walter" had brought the leaders together and provided an opportunity for an agreement to be reached.

Color television reportage brings us closer to events and involves us emotionally, often more than we wish. Much of the revulsion, and in time opposition, to the Vietnam War was probably a result of the repeated images on the television screen of the death and destruction in South Asian jungles. Vietnam, called "television's first war," engendered unexpected public reaction in America because of enhanced, immediate communication.

Terrorism and Television

The very nature of television and modern mass communication that can bring people close together while sharing the mutual grief and loss of tragic events, such as the assassination of John F. Kennedy or the funeral of Winston Churchill, also enables it to be manipulated to capture the world's attention. Unquestionably, certain acts of international terrorism, such as jet hijackings or political kidnappings and bombings, are perpetrated primarily to capture time and space in the world media. Terrorism has been called "propaganda of the deed": violent criminal acts (often against innocent people) performed by desperate people seeking a worldwide forum for their grievances.

Of course, terrorism is not new, but the flare-ups in the 1960s and 1970s—especially in the Middle East, Northern Ireland, Latin America, Italy, and West Germany—have been caused, some charge, by global television coverage that beams images of terroristic violence into millions of television sets around the world. Many terrorist groups have mastered a basic lesson of this media age: television news organizations can be manipulated into becoming the final link between the terrorists and their audience, and as with all sensational crimes, the more outrageous and heinous the terrorist act the greater attention it will receive in the world's news media. Professor Walter Laqueur has said: "The media are a terrorist's best friend. . . . Terrorists are the superentertainers of our time."[9]

Be that as it may, terrorism *is* news, and as such it poses worrisome questions for broadcast journalists: Does television coverage really encourage and aid the terrorists' cause? Is censorship of such dramatic events ever desirable? Professor Raymond Tanter of Michigan wrote: "Since terror is aimed at the media and not at the victim, success is defined in terms of media coverage. And there is no way in the West that you could not have media coverage, because you're dealing in a free society."[10]

Terrorism coverage is a journalistic problem of truly international scope, just as international terrorism itself is a transnational problem that individual nations cannot solve alone or without true international cooperation. Broadcast journalists argue about whether the violence would recede if television ignored or downplayed an act of terrorism. Most doubt that self-censorship by news organizations is a good idea or even possible in a highly competitive field; however, television organizations have established guidelines for reporting action in a more restrained and rational way.

Hostages in Iran

The seizure of the United States embassy in Iran in November 1979 and the holding hostage of more than 50 American citizens, virtually all diplomatic personnel, added a new and deepening dimension to the history of terrorism and the media's increasingly blurred role as both reporter and participant.

For the first time, a sovereign government became a party to the terrorism by supporting instead of ousting the young militants who, in contravention of recognized international law and custom, took over an embassy compound and imprisoned its personnel. Their stated purpose was to dramatize the grievances of Iranians against the deposed Shah Mohamed Reza Pahlevi and force the U.S. government to return him to Iran for trial. To get the U.S. media's attention (and the world's), the Iranians invited back the U.S. reporters they had earlier expelled. Visas were issued, coverage was unimpeded, transmission facilities were largely unrestricted, and even interviews were granted by Ayatollah Khomeini, the leader of the new Muslim state. Most observers agree that the militants and Iran's rulers expected the heavy print and television coverage of the outpouring of support of the terrorists by the huge, demonstrating crowds around the embassy gates would convince American and world public opinion of the justice of their cause. They had expectations, it is believed, that the dramatic pictures and reports, night after night in living color on the evening news, would do for them what coverage of the Vietnam War and the protests against it did for the antiwar movement in the United States in the late 1960s and early 1970s.

The saturation coverage of the year's biggest story quickly engulfed the U.S. news media, especially television, in controversy and brought charges that they were being used and manipulated by the Iranian militants. Particularly controversial was an interview by NBC News with an American hostage under conditions dictated by the Iranian captors, conditions both CBS and ABC had found unacceptable. The resulting criticism of NBC included such comments as: "NBC is the Benedict Arnold of broadcast journalism," and "The broadcast furthered the aims of Iranian terrorists." President Carter's press secretary, Jody Powell, called it "a cruel and cynical attempt" by Iran to divert public attention. NBC defended its broadcast as an "important public service."

For the more than 300 foreign journalists working in Teheran in the first months of the crisis, there was indeed a thin line between being manipulated by the Iranian militants and responding to legitimate demands from their own highly competitive news organizations and their publics at home for the latest information.

The prolonged crisis fomented charges of "media diplomacy." At a time of no official and few unofficial contacts between the two governments involved, journalists, often on camera, tried to commit Iranian officials to possible courses of action. U.S. State Department officials, striving to keep the situation fluid in order to facilitate negotiations, publicly criticized reporters for maneuvering Iranians into taking firm public stands. Several times, for example, journalists asked the foreign minister whether execution of the hostages was possible. The questioning caused considerable discomfort within the State Department.

Indisputably, the Western journalists in Teheran were part of the story and, inevitably, part of the controversy. The *New York Times* editorially came to the defense of television news:

American television, in doing its job, may at times serve Iranian Government purposes. It may at times serve American Government purposes. But throughout, it serves American *public* purposes as well. The public needs to understand Iranian passions, real as well as staged.

The public is not, in any case, so gullible as to swallow any Iranian argument whole; if anything, the various televised appearances of Iranian leaders have strengthened American resolve. . . . American journalists have not sought a diplomatic role in Iran. It has been thrust upon them. . . . The lesson is the same as always: the only duty the media can effectively perform is their own.[11]

The extent to which television has a responsibility for the effects of its coverage of such stories is a problem still to be resolved. Certainly, terrorism reportage highlights the fact that our ability to report a news event far outdistances our ability to understand it or control its impact.

Communication and Organization

A less obvious, more benign dimension of improved international communication is its capacity to *organize*. As Daniel Lerner has pointed out, communication is the neural system of organization.

Wherever people must act together (an informal definition of organization), there they must exchange information (an informal definition of communication). Communication, in the sense of shared information, is the organizing mechanism of social actions. . . . The proposition—that communication shapes organization—is applicable to all varieties of collective behavior in social institutions: large and small, formal and informal, hierarchal and egalitarian.[12]

The ability to communicate, in other words, determines the effectiveness and the boundaries of any organization. The growth in the nineteenth century of a continental nation such as the United States would have been impossible without the telegraph and the railroad—two media of communication that "organized" an expansive hinterland. Similarly, in the last part of the twentieth century, long-distance communication—including jet air travel and some surface transport, communication satellites, and high-speed telecommunications—is coalescing areas of the Third World previously isolated and splintered.

Although generally poor and deficient in modern communications, the continent of Africa, for example, has been transformed in recent years by its increased ability to communicate with itself. Because of greatly expanded air travel and long-distance communication between its capitals (but still not much between capital and adjacent hinterland), Africa is *organizing* itself. African leaders may often and loudly decry European influences on their continent, but it is precisely such "neocolonialist" influences as the BBC, INTELSAT, Air France, Reuters, *Le Monde*, AFP, *Newsweek*, and British Airways that have made possible the interaction and cooperation that has resulted in the Organization of African Unity and its numerous agencies and committees. Similarly, the shared policies and activities of black Africa directed at ending white rule in southern Africa would have been impossible without long-distance communication and jets. Comparable political changes throughout the world have been spawned by such communication advances, and at the same time, new communication technology is contributing to the widening of the gap between rich and poor nations. Would there be, for instance, the same sense of common cause and identification within the diverse Arab world stretching from Morocco to Iraq without greatly enhanced long-distance communication and jet travel?

Diffusion of Mass Culture

Another major aspect of the international communication system is its role in the diffusion of the mass culture of the West to remote parts of the world. Whether conveyed by printed word, electronic image, or recorded sound, Western motion pictures, television programs, popular music, books, and magazines have had an impact on traditional cultures around the world that can only be described as revolutionary. To the extent that we are moving toward a rudimentary world community, it can be argued that the world is beginning to share a common mass culture based on that of the West. The traditional cultures of diverse ethnic societies and nationalities are being steadily eroded and modified by this cultural intrusion principally from the United States and Britain.

For example, in 1976, gross billings and U.S. exports of motion pictures and television programs amounted to $700 million, with movies accounting for two-thirds of the total. *Reader's Digest* has attained the amazing foreign circulation of

12 million copies a month, and in the news area, over 200 newspapers outside the United States subscribed to either the New York Times or Washington Post-Los Angeles Times supplementary news services.

This has resulted in a love/hate relationship between many peoples around the world and the United States. The same persons who condemn the pervasive influence of American mass culture embrace things American—whether in dress, music, entertainment, or whatever. The young European or African intellectual who castigates America as a crass commercial influence will be a fan of U.S. popular music and movies, wear jeans, and follow the shifting trends of the American youth culture.

The explosion in international news communication is directly related to major scientific developments in computer technology and electronics; here, too, most of the developments have come from the West—mainly the United States—even though science and technology are perhaps the most truly international of activities.

Notes

1. Colin Cherry, *World Communication: Threat or Promise?* (New York: Wiley Interscience, 1971), pp. 57–58.
2. UNESCO, *World Communications* (Paris: UNESCO Press, 1975), p. 9.
3. Martin Woollacott, "Western News-gathering: Why the Third World Has Reacted," *Journalism Studies Review* 1, no. 1 (June 1976): 14.
4. *Wall Street Journal,* July 11, 1979, p. 1.
5. *Editor & Publisher,* September 29, 1979, p. 12.
6. *Wisconsin State Journal,* February 1, 1980, p. 14.
7. Jeremy Tunstall, *The Media Are American: Anglo-American Media in the World* (London: Constable, 1977), p. 23.
8. Ibid., p. 35.
9. Neil Hickey, "Terrorism and Television," *TV Guide,* August 7, 1976, p. 2.
10. Ibid.
11. *New York Times,* December 12, 1979.
12. Daniel Lerner, "Notes on Communication and the Nation State," *Public Opinion Quarterly* 37, no. 4 (Winter 1973–74): 541.

3

COMMUNICATION SATELLITES
AND NEW TECHNOLOGY

> IT would be difficult to overstate the magnitude of change that will take place in the lives of all of us, in human history, as a result of the information revolution that has so unobtrusively taken place in our day.
>
> —JOHN DIEBOLD
> *(authority on automation)*

THE presidential election of 1920 holds a place in communications history as the first in which election results were broadcast on radio. A crackling KDKA in Pittsburgh kept a small number of devotees of the new-fangled wireless in a small area of the country up to date on the tabulations as they slowly were counted.

But for large numbers of interested voters in the remote rural regions of America far from telegraph lines, without telephones, and beyond large population centers with daily newspapers, it took two weeks before the news reached them that Warren K. Harding had defeated James M. Cox for the presidency.

Sixty years later, there is not a spot in the United States—or in much of the world—where one cannot follow a presidential election tabulation instantaneously and, indeed, be told the winner's name even before all the polls close.

The drastic differences between then and now dramatize the fact that the mechanics of delivering the news to an interested public is a significant factor in the communication process. News, particularly international news, has over the years been directly affected by each new invention in communications. The telegraph, cable, telephone, and radio in turn have greatly extended the reach of foreign correspondents and the world news agencies and the speed with which they can deliver news, each innovation supplementing rather than replacing earlier methods of communication.

The pattern continues today with the latest and most revolutionary of technologies—communication satellites (comsats) and computer-based electronic methods of moving and storing information. Like many other institutions in American society, the news media—newspapers, news services, broadcast stations and networks, news magazines—are being strikingly altered by the computer revolution.

In our immediate concern with how international news moves about the globe, the significant changes launched by communication satellites cannot be ignored. Recently there has been a quantum jump in the ability of people to talk to and see one another.

The most immediate short-term effect of comsats is a reduction in the cost of long-distance communications and a corresponding increase in the number of words and pictures exchanged. In other words, more news will flow at less expense. The more dramatic changes are in long-distance telephone calls; they form the bulk of traffic on the INTELSAT system, which is operated by a multinational consortium controlling long-distance comsat communications. From 1950 to 1965, the number of overseas telephone calls made in the United States grew steadily; then the totals made a nearly vertical leap upward after the satellites became operational. By projecting current trends, within a few years an expected billion overseas telephone calls a year will be placed in the United States; and a call halfway around the world will cost the same as a call next door and be made almost as easily.

Another short-term but profound result, as both Peter Goldmark and Arthur Clarke have predicted, is that comsats, in combination with broadcast and cable television, will permit people to live where they please, regardless of their work. When cheap, dialed conversations by color television become commonplace, every house can be transformed into an office, theater, or classroom by pressing a few buttons.

In Clarke's view, such cheap communications will reverse the growth of the city. For him, the impact of comsats is a "slow but irresistible dispersion and decentralization of mankind. Megalopolis may soon go the way of the dinosaur."[1]

A projection by Professor Robert Jastrow of Columbia University is more chilling in the long term:

> The new satellites will provide a nervous system for mankind, knitting the members of our species into a global society. There are pluses and minuses. On the one hand, many lives will no doubt be enriched by freer exposure to ideas and people. Through the reduction of the barriers of fear and suspicion between nations, there may be greater political stability. On the other, a unified global society will be a social organism of great collective power, in which the individual plays the role of one biological cell in a complex organism. Just as a cell cannot migrate from, say, the brain to the liver, the freedom of the individual will tend to be restricted in the new society.
>
> The last comparable change in the history of life occurred several billion years ago, when multi-celled animals evolved out of colonies of individuals. The prospect is not pleasant. But the transformation, if it occurs, will take place slowly. Those now living will be dead before it is completed and most of our descendents will be conditioned to accept their more restricted options.[2]

Whether or not we agree with Jastow's somber view of the future, it is a reminder that people never fully appreciate the impact of new communication technology when it first appears. Clarke dismisses the notion that comsats are merely an extension of existing communication devices and will not evoke much change. He places comsats in the same class as the atomic bomb and automobile, "which represent a kind of quantum jump which causes a major restructuring of society." Clarke recalled a parliamentary commission in England a hundred years ago when the chief engineer of the post office was asked to comment on the need for the latest American invention, the telephone. The engineer made this remarkable reply: "No Sir. The Americans may have need of the telephone—but we do not. We have plenty of messenger boys."[3]

That telephone, in time, came to have its own revolutionary

impact on modern life, and the personal letter has been replaced by the long-distance call. And telephone services, as has been noted, constitute the primary activity today of communication satellites and are the major source of revenue for INTELSAT. At the end of the 1970s, the traffic of INTELSAT was still mostly people talking to people, but by 1985, INTELSAT officials project, at least half the volume will be machines communicating to other machines. In the years following, machines will be doing more and more of the "talking." The telephone is expected to continue to be a major tool of news gathering around the world for the rest of the century, but the comsat, as a by-product of the space age, has made a more dramatic entry into our lives than did the telephone.

Journalist Brenda Maddox warns:

It is easy to idealize and even to anthropomorphize the communications satellite. The usual kind of satellite rides 22,300 miles above the Equator, virtually equidistant from every country and every person within its enormous range. Only three are necessary to make a single television audience out of almost the entire globe. So small and so high, it seems to vault over the past, over mountains and oceans, and invites the whole world, jungle and suburb, to speak through it. The symbolic power of the satellite is so great that it is believed to have almost magical powers to educate, almost diabolical powers to persuade. The deep feelings that the device has aroused have bedeviled its short life. Planning for its orderly and effective use has been difficult and may become more so.[4]

Although they have been called microwave relay towers in the sky, comsats do have broader, unique properties. They do not link just two points, but many. They can receive from many places at the same time and transmit to many more, sending a panoply of message forms at once—television, telephone, telex, photo facsimile, and high-speed computer data. For example, an increased mobility of money is a result of the computer revolution. Computers and comsats have created a global financial marketplace, and it has been estimated that during a working day, "bits" of information about financial transactions representing as much as $100 billion is in transit along with all the rest of the traffic moving via satellite between Europe and North America.

Further, with comsats, distance is not a factor in the cost. Communications between Tokyo and Seattle, about 5,000 miles, and communications between Seattle and Portland, 175 miles, require identical facilities: two earth stations and a satellite. Irrelevant as well are the historic patterns of the world's communications, which were once channeled through the capital cities of the former colonial powers, all in the Northern Hemisphere. A telephone call from one African country to another had to go through London or Paris or both. In Latin America, a call between countries often had to go through New York or even London.

International journalism has benefited greatly from the developments that have made satellites an integral part of the communications industry. In 1980, satellite systems were operational at the international (intercontinental) level, the regional (continental) level, and the domestic (national) level. In addition, six military systems were functioning, as were systems designed for data relay and maritime and aeronautical purposes.[5]

INTELSAT is the largest and oldest system; as of 1980, some 102 nations belonged to the consortium, and any 2 members countries could communicate directly without going through a former colonial capital. As of March 31, 1979, INTELSAT also functioned as the carrier for national domestic services in 15 countries (Algeria, Brazil, Chile, Colombia, France, Malaysia, Nigeria, Norway, Oman, Peru, Saudi Arabia, Spain, Sudan, Uganda, and Zaire). Denmark, Egypt, India, and Iraq were also considering using the INTELSAT system.[6]

One of the first regional organizations, the 17-member-country European Space Agency (ESA), plans a European Communications Satellite (ECS) for digital communications and Eurovision in the 1980s. Other regional systems that are operational or imminently so include PALAPA 1 and 2 satellites serving Indonesia; Telesat's CTS and the ANIK series in Canada; the BSE 12/14 in Japan; and the Soviet-proposed Intersputnik's MOLNIYA 2 to link East Europe, Cuba, and Mongolia with Russia. The Symphonie 1 and 2 satellites, a joint venture of France and West Germany, has provided services since 1974–75. Other regional systems still being planned include ARABSAT, an Arab regional system; an African satellite system for the 38-member Panaftel group (AFROSAT); an Andean system to serve Brazil, Chile, Colombia, Ecuador, and Peru; and the NORDSAT system for the five Nordic countries.

International News by Comsats

Comsats have greatly expanded the capacity of the news media to move international news, but it is the ability of the satellites to relay color television signals (giving that medium an international impact) that has made comsat technology such a significant mass communication development. This is true, even though as recently as 1976, television use accounted for only 3 percent of the monthly revenue of INTELSAT.

When Early Bird, the first commercial comsat, was launched in 1965, the principal television use was expected to be for occasional live events such as sports, state funerals, space missions, and the coverage of disasters and wars. While coverage of such major events still accounts for much television traffic on INTELSAT, the most extensive and consistent use of the global system is for daily news "packages" sent from one country to another.

The U.S. networks—NBC, CBS, and ABC—almost daily incorporate satellite news feeds from their correspondents in various parts of the world or sporadically purchased special coverage from foreign broadcast systems.

Spain and Mexico became linked full time by satellite on a channel leased jointly by the two countries in 1975, and Spanish Television (TVE) in Madrid also transmits 10 or 15 minutes of news on weekdays to broadcasters in Argentina, Brazil, Chile, Colombia, and Venezuela. When events warrant, those countries send news by satellite back to TVE under what has come to be known as the Ibero-American News Exchange. Télédiffusion France (TDF) in Paris sends a daily package of news to Israel, Iran, Jordan, Martinique, the Ivory Coast, Gabon, Senegal, Zaire, French Guiana, Kuwait, and Saudi Arabia. In London, Visnews provides a daily news transmission to Australia, using the Indian Ocean satellite.

Comsats and computer-based data transmission have also greatly enhanced the capacity of the world news services to move written news around the world. Comsats have become an important supplementary channel along with cable, radio telephone, telegraph, and telex to disseminate major news. As a result, the international news flow, moving via electronic impulses from computer to computer at ever greater speeds, has markedly increased in volume. An Associated Press correspondent in Moscow can "type" a story into a video display terminal in AP's Moscow bureau, and the story can appear via comsat almost simultaneously on VDT screens in Paris, London, New York, Tokyo, Johannesburg, and Rome.

In today's worldwide news communication, a straight line is not the quickest route between two points. Take, for example, a major AP news story breaking in Kuala Lumpur, Malaysia. Say it involves a top Japanese personality, making it an important story in Tokyo but also of interest in the United States and elsewhere. The AP correspondent writes the story, and before the operator finishes transmitting the 200-word urgent lead from Kuala Lumpur via teleprinter, the story is being received in Tokyo and by AP members around the world.

Here is how the story is routed: Kuala Lumpur has an AP circuit that carries the story southeast to Singapore. From there it is automatically relayed northward via undersea cable to Hong Kong. Autorelay moves it again by undersea cable southeast to Manila, then eastward to a cablehead in San Francisco, and overland relay to New York. Circuit delay—i.e., lapsed time—is just one second. At New York, it is available to the AP "A" wire and for overseas relay to Europe.

Then, a New York computer turns the story around and sends it back via land lines and microwave to the earth-satellite relay station at Marysville, California. From there it is bounced off an INTELSAT IV satellite parked above the equator 22,500 miles over the Gilbert Islands in the South Pacific. The downward bounce from the comsat carries the story into Tokyo, seconds from the time it was transmitted from Kuala Lumpur. The story has traveled halfway around the world eastbound and back again westbound, racing from tropical Malaysia to wintry New York to the equator and again to chilly Tokyo.

AP's high-speed delivery of news, typical of the world services, has expanded steadily since 1961 when the old slow-speed barrier was broken by its DataSpeed transmissions of stock market tables at 1,050 words per minute. Faster delivery of general news copy began in 1975 with AP DataStream, which transmits 1,200 words per minute directly into clients' computers for entry into electronic editing systems. Then in May 1976, AP inaugurated a new service, AP DigitalStocks, which transmitted ten times faster than any existing system—12,000 words per minute. These new digital circuits transferred stock market tables from computer to computer, thus eliminating tape and tape-handling manpower in newspaper backshops. Such handling methods can move general as well as financial news across oceans as easily as across continents.

The individual daily newspaper receiving this rapidly disseminated material has been undergoing a parallel technological revolution based on computer technology and electronic data handling. The whole process of producing a daily newspaper has been speeded by moving electrons instead of words on paper. Typewriters, editing pencils, and paper have virtually disappeared from many newsrooms. A reporter now writes a news story on a video display terminal, which stores it in a computer until an editor calls it up at will onto his or her own VDT for editing. When the story is ready for printing, the editor presses a VDT button, and the story goes to electronically controlled machines that set it in type. Most daily newspapers can receive and process far greater amounts of editorial copy more quickly and at less expense than ever before. AP and UPI reports go directly into computers in newspaper offices. Hence there is expanded capacity to handle and print more international news, if editors are disposed to do so.

The speed and scope of foreign news reporting will be further expanded once portable VDTs are widely adopted. Foreign correspondents have long said that their worst problems are not censorship or other authoritarian restraints, but communications—getting to the remote news scene, such as an earthquake in Peru or a civil war in Angola, and then getting the story out. The technology to solve part of that problem has been developed: the Teleram P-1800 portable terminal with a magnetic tape cassette that can transmit stories directly to newsroom systems. Initially, the P-1800 was used to report golf matches, auto races, football and basketball games, and the Patricia Hearst trial.

AP reporters covering the Hearst trial wrote and edited their stories on P-1800 terminals located in the pressrooms of the San Francisco Federal Court House. Telephone lines were used to transmit the stories to a Hendrix 3400 editing system in the AP Los Angeles bureau. Essentially the same process could be used by foreign correspondents filing stories from remote regions via comsat hookups.

Another communication innovation that promises to be useful to the foreign reporter in the field is a portable wireless telephone. One prototype, the IMM UltraPhone, which weighs 45 ounces, has a range of up to 10 miles on the 450 mHz band and runs on a battery pack that will last up to 10 minutes for sending and 20 minutes for receiving. The unit can also be used to send and receive data for computer communications.

Telephone experts predict a significant expansion of mobile phone technology. Not only will there be phones in every car, but a cordless telephone to carry around in a pocket. A national or international telephone number for everyone then becomes feasible, with calls being forwarded automatically to the closest equipment. This means that an editor can telephone a foreign correspondent whether he or she is covering a conference in Geneva or an election in Spain. And that correspondent could, if necessary, send in the story by his or her cordless telephone.

Facsimile Newspapers

A further utilization of comsats that promises to be more momentous is facsimile production and distribution of national and even international newspapers. The *Wall Street Journal* has taken the lead in this new technology, which eventually may profoundly alter the structure of the daily newspaper business. This is the way it works: the *Journal* is put together at a production plant in Chicopee, Massachusetts. A facsimile of each page is then transmitted electronically to a satellite 22,300 miles above the equator. The satellite relays the page data to a *Journal* printing plant in Orlando, Florida, where it is received on page-sized photographic film. The sending and receiving of data, transmitted on equipment designed by American Satellite Corporation, takes about three minutes. Once the facsimile data is received, the photographic film is processed into offset plates. These plates then are placed on a newspaper press that can print up to 70,000 issues an hour for distribution in Florida and other parts of the Southeast. The same process occurs in a total of 12 printing plants serving the Midwest, Southwest, and West Coast regional editions. The *Wall Street Journal* has extended this expertise to Asia (see Chapter 4), and further expansion of the entire Dow Jones network (which includes the *Wall Street Journal*, the only truly national daily newspaper in America) is under way. This kind of technological innovation, plus an informative, well-written news product, has moved the *Wall Street Journal* into first place in circulation among U.S. dailies. In early 1980, the *Journal*'s circulation officially reached 1,775,000, putting it ahead of the *New York Daily News*.

Other publications routinely utilize facsimile transmission technology. For instance, the *World Journal*, a Chinese-language daily newspaper in New York City, is partially composed in New York and printed in San Francisco the same day. Again, full pages are transmitted via American Satellite network in minutes, and essentially the same paper is read by readers 3,000 miles apart.

Comsats are not necessary for facsimile production between distant points if surface means exist to handle the high-data-rate transmission necessary for high-speed facsimile movement. A famous Italian daily, the *Corriere Della Sera* of Milan, has a high-speed system that can transmit full-page, high-resolution proofs in six minutes or less per page from Milan to a subsidiary printing plant in Rome.

As early as 1974, the Paris-based *International Herald Tribune* began transmitting nightly the 14 to 16 pages of the newspaper to printers in Uxbridge, England, for printing and distribution in the United Kingdom. The transmission system was billed at the time as the first to cross national borders.

Such developments make the truly international or world-wide newspaper a technical reality, and in the foreseeable future, daily newspapers with a cosmopolitan outlook, such as the *Times* of London, *New York Times, Le Monde* of Paris, or the *International Herald Tribune,* will be available via comsat instead of by mail to readers in widely scattered places. In time, truly global daily publications could appear.

U.S. media interests recognize the potential of satellite communications for the news business, and in 1979, AP and UPI were granted permission to test satellite systems that would provide the basis for a shift from telephone lines to satellites as the primary links between wire services and their U.S. clients. AP then began implementing a large satellite distribution system of small-aperture, receive-only earth stations between 600 and 1,200 cities. When these stations are in place, the AP news report will move via a Western Union satellite more quickly and cheaply than before.

Is the Newspaper Becoming Obsolete?

These fast-moving changes in media technology raise the prospect that the daily newspaper itself may be headed for extinction. With the development of microcomputerization, the television set can become a kind of home encyclopedia, spewing out an almost limitless amount of written information including the day's news. Already in use in Europe are two major systems called teletext and viewdata.

Teletext utilizes the fact that the television broadcast signal that delivers a picture to a set does not use all the 525 lines of spectrum available. Thus 21 unused lines are harnessed by a central computer to transmit all kinds of print messages. Such data are invisible on the screen until the viewer employs a hand-held decoder to punch up teletext in place of usual programming. An example of teletext is the CEEFAX system developed by the BBC. CEEFAX permits any subscriber to call up a particular page of news onto his or her television screen at any time. Each page (a full television screen) can contain up to 120 words. The CEEFAX system has the capacity of 100 pages, but it can be adapted to transmit an unlimited number.

The CEEFAX operation begins in the news broadcast center. There, 120-word pages of news are assembled and typed into an electronic storage device. Each of the words on the page and the page number are digitally encoded automatically. The pages are then automatically transmitted sequentially in the blank spectrum space of a normal British television broadcast. Sixty-four pages of code take approximately 15 seconds to transmit and are repeated constantly four times a minute, hour after hour. Any or all the pages can be updated almost instantaneously. At the receiving end, in a home or office, the viewer can select any page desired. When the user punches, for example, page 23, the device waits until the next time page 23 is broadcast (maximum waiting time, 15 seconds), then displays it on the screen. Type size is about 18 point, and the page can be held on the screen as long as the viewer wishes.

In the late 1970s, KSL-TV in Salt Lake City began testing CEEFAX, adapting it to transmit 800 screen-size "pages" of information, which is equivalent to a 50-page newspaper.

Viewdata, on the other hand, employs telephone lines rather than broadcasting to deliver material, which is then stored in information banks. The early leader in this system is Prestel, which is being tested in London and elsewhere. The viewdata customer has the advantage of being able to call up any specific information desired. Prestel, in mid-1979, had 150,000 pages of computerized data available for subscribers, and the number of pages was expected to reach 9 million within five years.

An American competitor entered the field in June 1979 when UPI introduced its electronic home delivery service called UPI NewsShare. The news service can deliver newspaper editorial copy—UPI's worldwide news report—and classified by-products directly to the home via home computers. In 1979, an estimated 500,000 home microcomputers already were in use in the United States, and the number was increasing rapidly. UPI's full news report is delivered at high speed and stored in a computer at Silver Springs, Maryland. By dialing a local telephone number in most cities in the United States, home-computer users can contact the main computer and then ask for items of particular interest by punching simple codes on a key pad.

The first two major experiments in the United States on the "electronic newspaper" got under way in July 1980 and both used the viewdata method. The *Columbus* (Ohio) *Dipatch* began sending its entire editorial content to 3,000 home terminals around the country on a computer system. For $5 an hour, the home viewer could sit down at a computer keyboard and call up on the computer screen a list of all the stories appearing in the *Dispatch* that day. The viewer could select any article from a condensed index and read it or scan it, much as he would a newspaper spread out before him or her, and then go on to the next selection. The viewer also had access to AP articles, games, advertising, and other consumer services.

The other experiment was started by the Knight-Ridder Newspapers in Coral Gables, Florida. The $1.5 million project provided news, advertising, and other consumer services via 200 personal computers installed in area homes at no cost to participants. Thirty-one advertisers were part of the experiment. If viewers wanted to order goods from local stores, they typed messages into their terminals indicating what credit card they wanted the goods billed to and how and when they could like to have the items delivered.[7]

Such systems have important implications for international news. For in this era of long-distance telecommunications, an individual or a news medium can be located almost anywhere and still be able to request and obtain specific news and information from many miles away. But will such electronic information systems be a serious threat to conventional newspaper publishing? A study by the Arthur D. Little Company determined they will not be a threat in this decade, but by the mid-1990s they could substantially affect the news industry. Whether the impact is threat or opportunity will depend largely on the publishers, the study concluded. Those able to break away from their traditional roles as newspaper and magazine publishers and become broad-based "information providers" will find important additional channels for marketing their news and information services.

Implications of Rapid Change

To summarize, these innovations in communication technology suggest certain broad trends for transnational journalism:

1. The unit cost of international communication of news will continue to drop as usage of the world news systems increases and efficiency, speed, and reach of the hardware become greater.

2. Technology is making it possible to send and receive news and other essential information from almost anywhere in the world.

3. The two-way capability of cablevision, tied in with comsats and home computers, means that information receivers can seek out or request specific kinds of information or news and not remain a passive mass audience.

The two-way capability of telecommunications means that there is more likely to be a two-way flow of information, with receivers having more choice about what they receive. The trend toward such interactive communication systems is clear.

4. Because of technical improvements, the potential number of channels and sources of information is virtually unlimited, and the possible varieties and kinds of future communication stagger the imagination.

5. A gradual merger of the science and technology of computers and communications is now taking place. In fact, a new term, "compunications," has been coined to reflect this reality.

6. This communications (or compunications) revolution is essentially taking place in the West—principally the United States, Japan, and Western Europe. These "information societies"—all in the rich, industrialized North—are widening the already broad gap between themselves and the Third World. A highly industrialized nation like Japan can utilize any new technology much faster than, say, India, and as a result the frustrations and resentments of the Third World are exacerbated. The poorer nations want the new communications technology but lack the social and economic bases needed to use it. Such factors only add to the deep rift between the haves and have-nots of the world, a condition many consider the greatest of all global problems.

Concerned persons here and abroad are pondering the implications of all this. American newspaper publishers and other U.S. media people formed the International Press Telecommunications Council in the early 1970s to help assure the news media access to communication satellites. IPTC, which has British and Canadian members as well, has been concerned that new developments in computer-controlled data transmissions might increasingly restrict press telecommunications and international news flow in the years ahead.

John Forrest, IPTC chairman, told the group:

> One of the greatest problems facing both developed and developing societies is the great speed at which the technologies of the computer and communications are advancing. With the great mass of information that can now be assembled, processed, and disseminated through the technologies of the computer and modern telecommunications, mankind is now faced with the problem of having more and more facts in shorter and shorter periods of time.
>
> The advancing technologies of the developed societies are possibly now creating the seeds—I will not say of their own destruction—but are certainly creating massive problems for the societies which are developing the technologies. This especially applies to news dissemination.[8]

Society, in short, faces the danger of computer/communications technologies advancing faster than the ability to develop methods of controlling them and adjusting to their impacts. This has always been true of technologies, but today the gap is becoming ominously wide and is particularly evident in the attitudes of governments toward communications and international journalism.

Notes

1. Arthur Clarke, "Beyond Babel: The Century of the Communication Satellite," in *The Process and Effects of Mass Communication*, ed. W. Schramm and D. Roberts (Urbana: University of Illinois Press, 1971), pp. 952–65.
2. *New York Times*, June 9, 1974, News of the Week in Review section, p. 6.
3. Clarke, ibid.
4. Brenda Maddox, *Beyond Babel: New Directions in Communications* (Boston: Beacon Press, 1972), pp. 65–66.
5. Rolf T. Wigand, "The Direct Satellite Connection: Definitions and Prospects," *Journal of Communication* 30, no. 2 (Spring 1980): 140–41.
6. Ibid.
7. Deidre Carmody, "First U.S. Experiments in Electronic Newspapers Begin in Two Communities," *New York Times*, July 7, 1980, p. B 13.
8. Earl Wilken, "IPTC Considers Flexing Political Muscle," *Editor & Publisher*, June 4, 1977, p. 14.

4

INTERNATIONALIZING THE WORLD'S NEWS MEDIA

> MANKIND has become one, but not steadfastly one as communities or even as nations used to be, nor united through years of mutual experience . . . nor yet through a common native language, but surpassing all barriers, through international broadcasting and printing.
>
> —ALEXANDER SOLZHENITSYN

As the international flights put down in each capital in West Africa on Thursdays, one of the first cargoes unloaded are bundles of the international editions of *Time* and *Newsweek*. Within hours, the magazines have been distributed to news kiosks and hotel newsstands and into the hands of scores of newsboys, who hawk them on street corners and in cafes and bars.

By Friday morning, virtually all have been sold. They are much in evidence at the numerous gathering places in the towns, being read not merely, as one would expect, by white tourists or resident expatriates, but by equal, often greater, numbers of local citizens as well.

This weekly event is not peculiar to West Africa. It takes place in East Africa, too, and in similar ways in other spots around the globe—Asia, South America, Europe. Nor is the exclusive product *Time* and *Newsweek*. On Sunday afternoons, for instance, the newsboys most likely would be selling the Sunday papers from London: the *Sunday Times,* the *Sunday Telegraph,* and *News of the World.*

The appetite for such Western publications (most of them in English, which is becoming the lingua franca of international communication) is just one example of how all the major institutions of news communication—world news services, broadcast systems, great newspapers and magazines—have become internationalized in recent years. This change is the result in some instances of new technology and in others of shifting social and political realities. But whatever the cause, the fact is that more and more of the activities of the major news media now transcend parochial concerns and serve broader transnational purposes.

As worldwide institutions, the international news media share many of the attributes of multinational corporations, which have become such a powerful force in the postwar world economy. There has been much concern about the power and reach of these multinational corporations, largely because they appear to be exploiting certain nations and regions at the expense of others. Yet the burgeoning activities of such giants as Exxon, General Motors, Shell, Phillips, ITT, British Petroleum, Volkswagen, the great Japanese corporations, and lesser conglomerates are a creative and predictable response to the economic opportunities in the interdependent world in which we live. The solution is not just to curtail them but to regulate their activities in the interests of all. But without effective world government or even much international economic cooperation, effective regulation will be difficult, if not impossible, to accomplish.

Inability to regulate the world's economy fairly is another indication of the inadequacy of the nation state to deal with the world's truly international concerns.

The same kind of criticism leveled at multinationals is being directed at some transnational media. Charges have been made, for example, that great Western media institutions are becoming giant profit-grubbing multinational corporations exploiting poorer nations by dominating the news flow and dumping on them mass culture artifacts—television programs, movies, pop music records, magazines, and books—that disrupt local traditional cultures in the process. Included among such transnational media entrepreneurs would appear to be the U.S. television networks ABC, CBS, and NBC; the U.S. news agencies Associated Press and United Press International; Britain's British Broadcasting Corporation and Reuters; France's Agence France Presse; and surely the popular and much-imitated *Newsweek* and *Time* as well as the major motion picture and television distribution organizations.

Whether their activities are "good" or "bad" usually depends on the critic's personal tastes and ideology. But the internationalization of news media is proceeding in response to the needs of a shrinking world. The media are doing more than seizing the opportunities for greater profits from new markets, albeit those factors are obviously important. Whether viewed as another example of Western "media imperialism" or as a significant contribution to global understanding, more and more the international media are becoming increasingly cosmopolitan, speaking English, and catering to an internationally minded audience concerned about world problems.

"An American in Paris"

The daily, ink-on-newsprint newspaper is still the central institution of modern journalism, and there are more than 8,000 dailies worldwide. A few of the more serious "prestige" papers attract readers far beyond their national borders. Not many Americans read foreign publications, so they are unaware of the extent to which people abroad depend on newspapers and magazines published in other countries. The highly intellectual *Le Monde* of Paris, famous for its analyses of world affairs, is widely read in the Arab world and francophone Africa. Britain's *Guardian* and *Daily Telegraph* are found on many foreign newsstands, as are the *Frankfurter Allegemeine* and the *Neue Zürcher Zeitung* of Zurich. For example, the *Neue Zürcher Zeitung*, which celebrated its two hundredth anniversary on January 12, 1980, has a circulation of 120,000, about 20,000 of the total being copies sold abroad. Most of the paper's earnings are reinvested in the editorial department, which explains how a paper of that modest size can support 33 full-time foreign correspondents.

But the newspaper that has evolved furthest toward becoming a truly international daily is the *International Herald Tribune* of Paris. The *IHT* is the sole survivor of a number of English-language papers, including the *Chicago Tribune, Daily*

Mail (of London), *New York Herald-Tribune,* and *New York Times,* that published Paris or European editions for English-speaking travelers. Started by James Gordon Bennett in 1887 as the Paris edition of the *New York Herald,* the *IHT* has outlived its parent and today is jointly owned by Whitney Communications, the *Washington Post,* and the *New York Times.* The *IHT* is produced by an editorial staff of 40, including copyboys and clerks. About 90 percent of its copy comes from staffers on the *New York Times, Los Angeles Times, Washington Post,* and the news services. Averaging about 16 pages a day in 1981, the *Herald Trib* sells 130,000 copies a day in 143 countries, and no single country accounts for more than 15 percent of the total. Facsimile editions are printed in London and Zurich and a third location is being considered in the Middle East to reach its 10,000 Middle East readers. This marvel of distribution appears daily on some 8,500 newsstands all over Europe, with mail subscriptions throughout Africa and Asia.

In May 1980, the *IHT* announced it would begin printing an Asian edition in Hong Kong on September 15, 1980. Current *IHT* sales in Asia are 2,000 daily; within three years sales are expected to reach 20,000 daily. Same-day delivery of the Paris-based paper in most of Asia is to be accomplished by transmission of page images by satellite for reproduction in Hong Kong by Sing Tao Newspapers. This is the first time that satellite transmission of a complete newspaper will be accomplished on a daily basis from one continent to another.

Although it remains an American newspaper in outlook and perspective, it has gradually acquired an important non-American readership. Nearly half its readers are an elite group of European internationalists—businessmen, diplomats, and journalists fluent in English. These readers see the *IHT,* as do many Americans, as a superior newspaper: informative, balanced, literate, and well edited.

International Information Elite

These non-American readers are part of what William Read and U.S. government researchers have identified as an "international information elite" who, regardless of geographic location, share a similar rich fund of common experience, ideas, ways of thinking, and approaches to dealing with international problems. A U.S. Information Agency survey found, for example, that "on the average as many as 15 to 30 percent of selected elite audiences in non-Communist countries read *Time*."[1]

Read noted: "So when American media play an agenda-setting role globally, the effect can be to assign the degree to which international attention is focused on the issue. The energy crisis during the winter of 1973–74 dramatically demonstrated what can happen. When the Arabs turned off the oil in 1973, the whole world acted like a single short term market, because of simultaneous news coverage reaching people everywhere nearly simultaneously."[2]

USIA (now USICA) research concludes that the "information elites" have similar clusters of interests, principally international affairs and economics. To a lesser degree, they are concerned also about social problems but do not share a high interest in art and popular culture. The research indicates a "preference for substantially useful information related to a two-tiered world: global interdependence in politics and economics balanced against global diversity in cultural preferences."[3] A salient feature of the transnational elite audiences, Read wrote, is that they sit atop indigenous societies that are, in the main, highly nationalistic.

Numerous other publications, particularly magazines, have reached and helped shape this international information elite. The prime success story of transnational magazines is, of course, *Reader's Digest*, which established its first foreign edition in Britain in 1938. In time came 25 national editions printed in 13 languages in 22 foreign countries. The more than 11.5 million copies published abroad in 1974 reached about 50 million readers in every non-Communist part of the world. In some countries, including nearly all Spanish-speaking countries, the *Reader's Digest* was *the* most popular magazine.[4] So successful has been its adaptation to foreign soil that many readers are unaware that the *Digest* is not an indigenous publication. Although studies show that *Digest* readers abroad belong to a "quality audience" of the affluent, the well educated and the well informed, it is not that same audience of decision makers that read *Time* and *Newsweek*, which are primarily news media.

Time and *Newsweek*, besides spawning such notable imitations as *Der Spiegel* in West Germany and *L'Express* in France, have been quite successful as transnational publications and both can claim strong appeal to that internationally minded readership.

Time, over the years, has evolved into a multinational news medium for a multinational audience. Read pointed out that in mid-1975, when *Time*'s total circulation was about six million, *Time Canada*'s share was about 550,000, *Time Europe*'s (including Africa and Middle East), 458,000, the edition for the Pacific region, 369,261, and for Latin America, 136,136.[5] So 25 percent of *Time*'s copies are read abroad. Readership studies found that *Time*'s readers abroad are affluent, multilingual, cosmopolitan, and often a comparatively young business executive, who was "likely to be internationally oriented in his economic and political opinions."[6] *Time* has increasingly tailored the editorial contents of its regional editions to those readers' interests, and for advertisers abroad, the magazine has offered more than 60 different editions based on geography.

Newsweek has done much the same thing overseas. In 1972, *Newsweek International* announced a major expansion and boasted that during the year it ran hundreds of exclusive stories and featured 22 covers different from the domestic edition. While *Time* has tailored its overseas editions to regional interests, *Newsweek* has tried to be more global in its approach. Only 15 percent of its readers abroad are Americans; the rest are from 150 countries. *Newsweek* has always had signed columns, but American columnists rarely appear in the international edition. Instead, the magazine publishes another team of internationalists whose members include journalists from Australia, Italy, Britain, Indonesia, West Germany, France, Japan, and Sri Lanka.

Another American competitor of the news magazines abroad appeared in 1976 with the debut of the *Asian Wall Street Journal*. With a satellite-assisted leap across the Pacific, the highly successful *Journal* launched an Asian edition in Hong Kong that covers a 16-country, 6,000 square mile business beat from Manila to Karachi. Averaging 12 pages, one-third the size of the domestic edition, the Asisan edition tries for the same mix of authoritative business and political news, a risky experiment for a region with so little press freedom.

The *Journal's* new enterprise is only possible because of space-age technology. With a small Asian-based staff of writers and editors, the paper relies on the resources of its domestic organization. The *Journal* transmits more than a 40,000-word file of stories and headlines from New York to Hong Kong in just under six hours daily. This material is re-edited and then printed in time to make the midday airline flights to other Asian capitals. The copy from New York is sent at 1,000 words a minute via high-speed computers using satellite circuits, then is converted from computer tapes directly into paste-up columns for photo-offset.

The *Asisan WSJ* is edited for the same international information elites who read *Time* and *Newsweek*. By the beginning of 1980, the circulation had reached 19,000, but the paper was expected to continue losing money for another two years.

Almost anywhere one travels abroad, stacks of foreign publications can be found on newsstands, especially in Third World countries. A traveler arriving in francophone Abidjan, the capital of the Ivory Coast, is impressed to find almost all the major French magazines plus that day's editions of the Paris dailies, all flown in by jet. Similarly, in Nairobi, Kenya, a choice of British papers, including same-day delivery of the Sunday papers, is available at hotels and newsstands. This plentitude of reading matter may represent unfair competition with the struggling local press, but these publications do provide a window on the world for that small but essential group of influentials who want to be informed about world affairs.

Changes in News Services

The subtle changes in the world news services as they have expanded in postwar years is further evidence of this growing internationalization of transnational media. Although they claim to "cover the world," the agencies historically have tended to serve primarily their own national clients and those in their spheres of influence; i.e., Reuters serviced British media and the British Commonwealth, AFP, the French press and overseas French territories, and UPI long had strong connections in Latin America. But these world agencies have become more international in scope, selling their services to whoever will buy wherever they may be. UPI, for example, has a French language service that competes with AFP for provincial French newspapers and for clients in francophone Africa. AFP is now used in many countries of the British Commonwealth. AP is so widely used in Germany that it is practically a German service and a strong competitor to Deutsche Press Agentur (DPA).

In addition, the personnel of world agencies have become significantly internationalized. Formerly, the AP, for example, boasted that its news from abroad was reported by American AP correspondents who had experience in running an AP bureau in the United States. The agency would not depend on foreign nationals to provide news from their own countries for AP use in the United States. Now that has changed. With the increased professionalism of journalists abroad, news agencies not only find it more economical to use qualified local journalists but often get better reporting from those who know their own country, its language, and its social and political traditions.

Today only about one-tenth of AP's 800 employees abroad are U.S. citizens, and these latter are better prepared in language training and international studies than their predecessors a generation earlier. Three of AP's five Pulitzer Prizes for Vietnam War reporting went to Peter Arnett, a New Zealander, Horst Fass, a German, and Huynh Cong Ut, a Vietnamese. UPI maintains a multinational staff overseas that includes two senior executives with British and French citizenship.

Nevertheless, ties to their own national media clients remain strong (no overseas client can be a member of the AP cooperative), and the news values of these clients are of major importance in deciding news priorities, even though it makes sense for a world news agency to sell its services as widely as possible. For example, the more customers there are in Latin America for UPI, the easier it is for UPI to collect Latin American news, and, in turn, the greater the incentive not only to send that news to

American clients but also to distribute it among Latin American clients. Although the world news agencies are accused of neocolonial domination of news flow to and from the Third World, the fact remains that these highly competitive services *sell* their news reports, and to make them saleable or useful to editors and broadcasters abroad, a news agency must present news that editors abroad are interested in using. Furthermore, in many Third World nations, world news agency reports are sold directly to national or official news agencies, which redistribute them to local media.

For notwithstanding the expansion of the world agencies since 1945, some 120 national and regional news agencies now operate, mostly in the newly independent nations of the Third World. Usually official or government controlled, they function mainly to collect and disseminate news within their own boundaries for their own media and to exchange news with the world news agencies. The Ghana News Agency, for example, supplies news about Ghana to Reuters, which has no correspondent in Ghana, and Reuters, in turn, sends the Reuters' Africa Service to the Ghana News Agency for redistribution to local media.

Numerous efforts have been made in recent years to organize these national agencies into continental or regional services to compete effectively with the world agencies. So far the efforts have not been notably successful and will be discussed in a later chapter.

Another facet of internationalization is foreign syndication of news by major daily papers. The U.S. leader has been the New York Times News Service, which sends 40 to 50,000 words daily to about 130 papers abroad. The closest competitor is the Washington Post/Los Angeles Times News Service, which transmits 20,000 words to about 100 foreign papers. Some major European papers also sell their news and features abroad. Subscribers to this supplemental news are mostly the larger and more prestigious papers, especially in Western nations, which use the syndicated material to supplement other sources.

As noted previously, there is syndication also of television news film and videotapes, especially those of America's NBC, CBS, and ABC and Britain's BBC, most of it distributed by two Anglo-American firms—Visnews and UPITN—via videotape and satellite to almost every television service in the world. There is probably more international cooperation than competition in the transnational video film business because most nations have only one government-controlled television service. Jeremy Tunstall has described the Visnews operation:

> In addition to its core of BBC, NBC, and NHK (Japan) news-film, Visnews has its own staff of television reporters and stringers around the world. On any day it has about 30 video stories of which some 8 or 10 are sent to any individual television client. At Visnews headquarters in west London not far from Heathrow Airport, it is possible to see set out on just two sheets of paper a table indicating which of today's video stories are going to which of the 193 customers in 98 countries and territories of the world. Of the 12 or 15 minutes sent each day to each client, the typical television network used 4 or 5 minutes each day on its news bulletins, whilst some poorer television networks used the full 12 to 15 minutes day after day.[7]

Unlike in the print media, which carry a credit line on agency reports or syndicated material, syndicated television news is usually presented anonymously. Whether watching in New Orleans or Nairobi, the viewer is rarely told who supplied the foreign video news. Therefore, most viewers around the world are unaware that Visnews and UPITN dominate the distibution so completely.

Increased communication, as had been stressed earlier, leads to increased organization and consequently some concentration of control in the international news media. Fewer and fewer editors and broadcast executives are making editorial decisions for more and more people. The need to cooperate and join together in organizations seems at times stronger than the demands of independence and competition. Regional and continental media organizations are playing increasingly crucial roles in international news communication.

A prime example of such supranational cooperation is the European Broadcasting Union (EBU), which has developed some highly regarded news exchanges on Eurovision. (London is a major video news center in part because it is has the advantage of membership in the Eurovision New Exchange.)

The first proposals for the Eurovision News Exchange (EVN) were made in 1957, and after limited experience in 1958–59 among 8 countries, a daily exchange began in 1960.[8] Today this unusual example of international journalistic cooperation extends from Western to Eastern Europe, North and South America, North Africa, and the Middle East. The EVN affords rapid access to news stories produced daily by the national television services and newsfilm agencies of the 22 countries of Western Europe, North Africa, and the Middle East, which are full members of the EBU.

Charles Sherman, who studied the EVN operation closely, wrote:

The EVN is an outstanding example of international pragmatism and cooperation. It illustrates how professional news and interests can readily unite diverse cultures and personalities in joint action. While the EVN may serve some altruistic purposes, it was only established to provide members with a rapid and efficient means of transporting highly perishable news items. It can deliver its cargo almost instantly from one country to another without being delayed by customs, bad weather, or other obstacles faced by systems which physically transport newsfilm.[9]

Similar organizational feats have been achieved by the International Radio and Television Organization (OIRT) headquartered in Prague and serving the Intervision network of East European television outlets. Although their activities and purposes vary greatly, the roster of international broadcasting organizations is impressive: the Union of National Radio and Television Organizations of Africa (URTNA), the Asian Broadcasting Union, the Inter-American Association of Broadcasters, the Commonwealth Broadcasting Conference, and the International Telecommunications Union (ITU). Among print organizations, the International Press Institute and the Inter American Press Association are the most important of the non-Communist, nongovernmental organizations. The IPI and IAPA enable independent newspapers to respond in a coordinated and often effective way to international threats to freedom of the press.

The main point of all this is that the news media of individual nations working through international organizations are going through subtle institutional changes even though considerable provincialism, touched by nationalistic concerns, still permeates their activities. Much of the activity of these international media organizations does concern broader, transnational purposes, and that is important.

Some argue, however, that these evolutionary changes in world media organization are coming too slowly. Henry R. Cassirer of UNESCO has said that as technology transcends national boundaries in the era of space communications, there is an inevitable urge toward new forms of organization to meet the challenge of world society.

Cassirer wrote:

This world will require a new organization of the communications media so they may serve the whole of mankind, a form of world communication to supplement others that exist, and will continue to exist, at the national and local level. The flow of information and comment, the dialogue between divergent forces, the spread of education and cultural cross-fertilization call for productions conceived in content and form not only from a national but also from a universal point of view. Eurovision and Intervision, the worldwide relay of television programs from the Olympic Games or from the moon, are first steps in this direction. But they suffer from a double limitation: They are subject to agreements between independent national broadcasting organizations, and they are centered largely around special events of a more or less spectacular nature. Yet technology and global interdependence make it both possible and urgent to envisage continuous programming for a world audience. . . . Inevitably and painfully, public policy will strive toward world-wide public broadcasting.[10]

English as Media Language

Increased communication across national borders naturally requires that sender and receiver communicate in a mutually understandable language. More and more that language is English, which is clearly the leading tongue of international communication today. Among the "Big Ten" of world languages, English ranks second with 380 million speakers after Mandarin Chinese with 690 million and is ahead of Russian with 259 million speakers, Spanish with 238 million, Arabic with 142 million, and German with 120 million. Furthermore, English is more widely used geographically, and for many millions of educated persons around the world it is their second language. In Europe, English is the most popular second language among younger people. An estimated 600 million speak it either as a primary or secondary language and can therefore be "reached" through English. What is more, this number includes most of the world's leaders. Unquestionably, English has become the global language of science and technology, with half the scientific literature of the world and most computer programs in English. For many Third World nations, English is the language of education, providing an entrée to knowledge and information. (But one unfortunate result is that many who speak English, especially Americans, have much less incentive than, say, Israelis, Dutch, or Swedes to learn other peoples' languages. Few of us even learn to speak Spanish, although it is widely spoken here and is the first language of more than 20 million native-born U.S. citizens.)

For these and other reasons, English has also become the leading media language in international communication. Most of the world's news—whether by cable, shortwave radio, telex, telegraph, or comsats—is carried in English. Not only AP, UPI, Reuters, and Visnews but also AFP, DPA, and even TASS transmit some of their news in English, as do many national news agencies.

Moreover, English is the leading linguistic medium in a major field of world communications: shortwave radio broadcasting targeted to audiences in foreign countries. A total of 100 broadcasting outlets with central studios in 84 countries use English as a means of reaching listeners beyond their national frontiers.

Some of the leading shortwave broadcasters and their daily English-language broadcasts are:[11]

COUNTRY	HOURS DAILY IN ENGLISH
China	19
East Germany	10
Great Britain	34
Japan	13
Netherlands	12
Philippines	11
Sri Lanka	11
USSR	27
USA: Voice of America	31
Armed Forces Network	24

The imperialism of nineteenth-century Britain was a major reason, of course, why so many people from Singapore to India to Kenya to Nigeria to Bermuda converse today in English. Not unrelated is the phenomenon of the many English language daily newspapers flourishing today in countries where English is neither the official nor even the most widely used language. Beginning with the *Chronicle of Gibraltar* in 1801, English language dailies, catering to expatriates, the foreign community, and local educated elites, have long survived, if not always flourished, in such diverse cities as Mexico City, Caracas, Paris, Rome, Athens, Cairo, Beirut, Manila, Bangkok, Singapore, and Tokyo as well as throughout India and Pakistan and the former British territories of Africa such as Nigeria, Ghana, Sierra Leone, Uganda, Kenya, Tanzania, and Zambia. In parts of polyglot Africa, English has almost evolved into another African language because of the role it plays in education, commerce, and mass communication.

Most of the artifacts of mass culture that move across national borders are in English. Tunstall said that English is the language best suited for "comic strips, headlines, riveting first sentences, photo captions, dubbing, sub-titling, pop songs, bill boards, disc-jockey banter, news flashes, sung commercials."[12]

English, the most widely spoken language of Western Europe, is fast becoming a lingua franca of the Communist countries of Eastern Europe. In Poland and Czechoslovakia, words like "trip," "smoke," "car," "dance," "gag," and dozens of others are part of young people's vocabulary. "English for You" is one of the most widely followed language courses on East German television, and English courses at evening schools are invariably overfilled.

Young East Germans, Czechs, and Hungarians, like the early postwar generation of West Europeans, tend to pick up their vernacular English from English-language broadcasts on Radio Luxembourg and the American Armed Forces Network. They avidly memorize the texts of popular songs, a method the BBC has adopted for one of its language courses beamed abroad. For the East European, as for the West African or the South Asian, English becomes essential for links to the outside world.

This thrust of English as a world media language has become self-generating, and any educated person of whatever nationality who wishes to participate in our shrinking and interdependent world must understand English. In fact, since English is now spoken by more non-English than English or Americans, it must now be considered as belonging to the world, as indeed it does. For when two persons of differing linguistic backgrounds are able to converse, the chances are they will be speaking in English.

The English language has been described as the greatest neocolonialist force in the world today. Perhaps in some contexts it is, but more importantly, English is the principal language in which the world communicates with itself.

Notes

1. William Read, *America's Mass Media Merchants* (Baltimore: Johns Hopkins University Press, 1976), p. 14.
2. Ibid., p. 15.
3. Ibid.
4. Ibid., p. 136.
5. Ibid., p. 121.
6. Ibid., p. 124.
7. Jeremy Tunstall, *The Media Are American: Anglo-American Media in the World* (London: Constable, 1977), p. 36.
8. Charles E. Sherman and John Ruby, "The Eurovision News Exchange," *Journalism Quarterly* 51, no. 3 (Autumn 1974): 478.
9. Ibid., p. 485.
10. Henry R. Cassirer, "Communicaitons—Key to Man's Self-Awareness," *Environment and Society in Transition,* vol. 84 (New York: New York Academy of Sciences, 1971), pp. 314–15.
11. Richard E. Wood, "English in International Broadcasting," *English around the World,* no. 15 (November 1976), p. 1.
12. Tunstall, *Media Are American,* p. 128.

5

CLASHING IDEOLOGIES:
FIVE CONCEPTS OF THE PRESS

A journalist is a grumbler, a censurer, a giver of advice, a regent of sovereigns, a tutor of nations. Four hostile newspapers are more to be feared than a thousand bayonets.

—NAPOLEON BONAPARTE

Abuses of the freedom of speech ought to be repressed, but to whom dare we commit the power of doing it?

—BENJAMIN FRANKLIN

THE gadgets and hardware of the new technology and the news media that utilize them have no control over how the reports of the events of the day emerge from the global news prism, whose planes and surfaces have been hewn and polished by diverse and frequently antagonistic political and social systems. As the news passes through the prism, one person's truthful, objective reporting can bend into what becomes distortion or propaganda to another.

For despite our extensive technological expertise, human controversies and cultural conflicts prevent the international news process from working smoothly and harmoniously. More and faster news communication across national borders does not automatically lead to better understanding; often it results in enmity and distrust, since the profound cultural and social differences that characterize the world community preclude agreement on what is legitimate news.

As a result, international journalism in recent years has been the subject of increasing rancor and mutual hostility and suspicion. Mass communication's powerful ability to publicize, to expose, to glorify, to criticize, to denigrate is universally recognized and often feared. At one time or another, government officials in every land become unhappy or dismayed with the press and often do something about it. In the West, a president or prime minister may complain bitterly that his or her programs are unfairly reported by press opponents. In a central African country, an offending Associated Press correspondent may be thrown into jail and beaten by the nation's dictator himself, as actually happened in the former Central African Empire.

These differing perceptions about the nature and role of news are rooted, of course, in divergent political philosophies and historical traditions and are reflected in five political concepts of the press found in the world today: (1) Authoritarian concept; (2) Western concept; (3) Communist concept; (4) Revolutionary concept; and (5) Developmental (or Third World) concept.[1] These contrasting approaches to the role and function of transnational journalism can help us understand some of the issues that divide the world's press.

Authoritarianism is the oldest and most pervasive concept and has spawned two twentieth-century modifications: Communist and Developmental. The Western concept, under which the press in Western parliamentary democracies functions, represents a fundamental alternative to the Authoritarian concept and contains elements of both eighteenth-century libertarianism and twentieth-century views of social responsibility. Revolutionary concept has one trait in common with the Western; they both try to operate outside of government controls.

Newspapers and other mass media, always and everywhere, function within various forms of governmental, societal, and economic restraints. Even the "freest" or most independent press system must deal with varying degrees of regulation by authority. In the relationship between government and mass communication, the basic question is not whether government controls the press, but the extent of those controls, for all press systems exist on a continuum from complete controls (authoritarianism) at one end to relatively few controls (libertarianism) on the other. Absolute freedom of expression is a myth. Beyond that, controls on the press are so varied and complex that it is difficult, if not impossible, to compare the freedom of the press in one nation with that in another. In one country, newspapers may be under harsh, arbitrary political restraints; in another, they may be under more subtle yet real economic and corporate restrictions.

A basic tenent of this analysis is that all press systems reflect the political and economic systems of the nations within which they operate. For the trend toward internationalization notwithstanding, print and broadcast systems still function within the structures of national political entities. And in this era of transnational communication, journalists from an open society often must work and collect news in a closed or autocratic society, thereby increasing opportunities for collisions between divergent concepts.

Authoritarian Concept

Authoritarianism was in effect at the time the printing press was invented by Gutenberg in the midfifteenth century, and in the years since, more people have lived under an authoritarian press than under any other. The basic principle of authoritarianism is quite simple: the press exists to support the state and authority. A printing press cannot be used to challenge or undermine the ruler. The press functions from the top down; the king or ruler decides what shall be published because truth is a monopoly of those in authority.

There is much in Western philosophy, developed over many centuries, that stresses the central importance of authority in political theory. From Plato's *Republic* through Hobbes's *Leviathan* to Hegel and Marx, the all-powerful state is given both the right and duty to sustain and protect itself in any way necessary.

To the authoritian, diversity is wasteful and irresponsible, dissent an annoying nuisance and often subversive, and consensus and standardization are logical and sensible goals for mass communication. There is compelling logic behind this.

As the eighteenth-century Englishman, Dr. Samuel Johnson, wrote:

> Every society has a right to preserve public peace and order, and therefore has a good right to prohibit the propagation of opinions which have a dangerous tendency. To say the magistrate has this right is using an inadequate word: it is the society for which the magistrate is the agent. He may be morally and theologically wrong in restraining the propagation of opinions which he thinks dangerous but he is politically right. [2]

To many in authority around the world today, these views are not unreasonable, certainly not to leaders of poverty-stricken developing nations faced with monumental tasks of political integration and economic development. Why, under such circumstances, should government tolerate what it considers disruptive and seditious views? Why should it permit foreign journalists to enter its country and then write critical and negative reports to the outside world, undermining the authority and prestige of the rulers?

Under traditional authoritarianism, the press is outside of government and is permitted to gather and publish news, but it operates for the "good of the state." The government leaves the press alone as long as it does not criticize authority or challenge the leadership in any way. If the press does attack authority, then the government intervenes, imposing censorship or even closing down publications and jailing editors. Under the Authoritarian concept, there is always the constraint of potential censorship, if not actual prior restraint itself. Editors and reporters never know for sure just how far they can go without triggering official disfavor and intervention. They must maintain the status quo and not advocate change or alternate leadership.

So wherever governments arbitrarily intervene and suppress independent newspapers and broadcasters, there the Authoritarian concept flourishes. Authoritarianism is widespread today, especially if the Communist and Developmental concepts are understood to be variations of traditional authoritarianism. Western journalists often encounter a variety of difficulties when reporting about authoritarian countries—entry visas are denied;

stories are censored; telex and comsat facilities are refused; and sometimes they are harassed, mistreated, jailed, or expelled.

Western Concept

The Western concept represents a democratic deviation from the traditional authoritarian controls. The long constitutional struggle in Britain and the United States slowly evolved a press relatively free of arbitrary government controls. In fact, one definition of freedom of the press is the right of the press to report, comment on, and criticize government without retaliation or threat of retaliation from that government. This been called the "right to talk politics." Historically, seditious libel meant criticism of government, laws, or officials. The absence in any country of seditious libel as a crime has been regarded as the true pragmatic test of freedom of expression, since politically relevant speech is what press freedom is all about.

By this demanding test—the right to talk politics—the Western concept is comparatively rare in today's world, although many authoritarian governments give it lip service. A free or independent press is usually found in only a handful of Western nations that share these characteristics: (1) a system of law that provides meaningful protection to individual civil liberties (here common law nations such as the United States and Britain seem to do better than nations like France or Italy, with civil law traditions); (2) high average levels of per capita income, education, and literacy; (3) governance by multiparty, parliamentary democracy or at least with legitimate political oppositions; (4) sufficient capital or private enterprise to support media of news communication; and (5) an established tradition of independent journalism.

Any list of nations meeting these criteria for a Western press today would certainly include the United States, the United Kingdom, Canada, Sweden, West Germany, France, The Netherlands, Belgium, Australia, New Zealand, Norway, Denmark, Austria, Iceland, Ireland, Israel, Italy, and Switzerland. In addition to these Western nations, highly developed and westernized Japan would be added.

Journalists in many other nations support and practice the Western concept, but because of political shifts, their press swings back and forth between freedom and control. Such places include Spain, Greece, Portugal, India, Colombia, Sri Lanka, Turkey, and Venezuela.

By and large, the Western nations that meet the criteria include the handful that do most of the world's news gathering from other nations and whose correspondents most often come in conflict with authoritarian regimes. For the Western concept holds most strongly that the government—any government, here or abroad—must not interfere in the process of collecting and disseminating news. The press, in theory, must be independent of authority and, of course, exist outside of government as a Fourth Estate and be well protected by law and custom from arbitrary government interference. Not many journalists in the world work under such conditions.

The ideals of Western journalism are a by-product of the Enlightenment and the liberal political tradition reflected in the writings of John Milton, John Locke, Thomas Jefferson, and John Stuart Mill. Primarily, there must be a diversity of views and news sources available—a "marketplace of ideas" from which the public can choose what it wishes to read and believe. For no one or no authority, spiritual or temporal, has a monopoly on truth. Judge Learned Hand said it best:

That [newspaper] industry serves one of the most vital of all general interests: the dissemination of news from as many different sources, and with as many different facets as is possible. . . . It presupposes that right conclusions are more likely to be gathered out of a multitude of tongues than through any kind of authoritarian selection. To many this is, and always will be, folly; but we have staked upon it our all.[3]

Underlying this "self-righting" process is the faith that citizens will somehow make the right choices about what to believe if enough voices are heard and government keeps its hands off. In the international context, it means there must be free flow of information unimpeded by any intervention by any nation. No government anywhere should obstruct the gathering of legitimate news.

This is not to say that Western news media are without shortcomings—serious ones. Political freedom does not preclude economic and corporate controls and interference with journalistic practices. A privately owned media system will, in varying degrees, reflect the interests and concerns of its owners.

To stay independent of outside controls, including government, the media must be financially strong and profitable. But journalistic excellence and profitability are not identical goals, although some of the best news media are also very profitable; for some owners, however, making money is the primary purpose of journalism, and independence and public service mean little.

Furthermore, diversity at both national and international levels appears to be in decline, and the increase of media monopolies and ownership concentration has reduced the number of independent voices heard in the marketplace. More and more newspapers, magazines, and broadcasting stations are becoming parts of huge media conglomerates. In some democracies, such as Norway and Sweden, the government maintains diversity of political views by providing subsidies to the newspapers of the various political parties, a practice not without a potential danger to press independence.

Some modifications in the Western concept fall under the rubric of social responsibility. This holds that the media have clear obligations of public service that transcend moneymaking. Public service implies professional standards for journalists as well as for fair and objective reporting. The media are obligated, in addition, to insure that all voices and views in the community are heard. Further, government is granted a limited role in intervening in media operations and in regulating conditions if public interests are not being adequately served. Government regulation of broadcasting in Western nations offers a good example of the social responsibility position.

Thus, in the Western concept, the media have a positive responsibility to provide reliable and essential information from around the world. By so doing, journalists help protect political liberty by providing information that a democratic society requires if it is to govern itself.

Communist Concept

In some places in the world, the Western concept is regarded as a culture-bound by-product of industrialized capitalist nations irrelevant to the needs and problems of Socialist and Developing nations. Furthermore, it is considered fallacious to judge the non-Western press by Western standards.

Lenin maintained that a press always served the dominant (ruling) class. Therefore, he concluded, access to the press must be denied to certain unsupportive elements of society, and freedom of the press consisted not so much in the right to say what one wished but in controlling the economic structure of the press—in short, newsprint, printing equipment, and buildings.

As the thinker most responsible for articulating the Communist concept, Lenin once wrote:

Capitalists call "freedom of the press" that state of affairs when censorship is removed and all parties are free to publish any newspapers. In this very thing there is no freedom of the press but freedom to deceive the oppressed and exploited mass by the rich, the bourgeoisie. "Freedom of the press" of a bourgeois society consists in freedom of the rich systematically, unceasingly, and daily in the millions of copies to deceive, corrupt, and fool the exploited and oppressed mass of the people, the poor.[4]

In the Communist view, a free and independent press becomes a divisive, costly luxury that does not serve the needs of the state and hence the people. Mass media controlled and directed by the state can concentrate on the serious task of nation-building by publishing news relating to the entire society's policies and goals determined by the top party leadership. Lenin saw the press's first function to be an organizing instrument to inform and control a revolutionary party apparatus seeking to overthrow a government. To him the press was an integral part of the Communist party, which was itself seen as a teacher to instruct the masses and lead the proletariat.

The press and broadcasting are perceived as instruments, along with other institutions such as schools and labor organizations, with which to rule. The press is "agitator, propagandist, and organizer." Media serve as implements of revelation (by revealing purposes and goals of party leaders) as well as instruments of unity and consensus.

Essentially, the Communist concept differs from the traditional authoritarian view in that the communication media become state owned, not privately owned, and serve a positive function of helping the government to rule. The press is required to do something, not merely avoid offending the rulers. In the Soviet Union and in other nations of the Communist commonwealth such as East Germany, Poland, Hungary, China,

Bulgaria, Czechoslovakia, and Rumania, the press is integrated into the monolithic Communist state. Whereas the Western libertarian views press freedom as freedom *from* government, the Communist concept regards it as freedom *within* the all-powerful state to pursue the goals of the state.

It is ironic that although the Soviet press was conceived in theory and matured in practice as a subversive and revolutionary instrument before the 1917 Revolution, it reached full maturity under Stalin and has since become in postwar Eastern Europe an instrument of conformity and consensus while still espousing Lenin's revolutionary ideology. The elaborate press system of the Soviet Union and its Socialist neighbors has become, in actual practice, a conservative caretaker of the status quo, a staunch supporter of long-standing Communist regimes. No attention is given in the Soviet media to the views of dissidents and advocates of radical or revolutionary change. The efforts of Western journalists to report the views of Soviet dissidents, a good news story by Western standards, is much resented by Soviet authorities and considered as serious interference in their internal affairs. As Lenin said, there is no freedom for enemies of the state.

Implicit in the Communist concept is the conviction that the Communist party must maintain a monopoly on all mass communication. Communist regimes have never been particularly hospitable to Western journalists. During the Stalin years, the few foreign reporters admitted faced censorship, visa problems, restricted access and travel, etc. Few Western publications were permitted through the Iron Curtain, and radio broadcasts to Eastern Europe were jammed. In recent years, the Communist regimes have worked out a modus vivendi of sorts with Western reporters, and things are more open than before. The gathering of news in Communist societies, however, remains difficult and demanding; Western journalists are still harassed on occasion.

Since the death of Mao Zedong, the People's Republic of China—that other great Communist nation—has become more accessible to foreign reporters. Bureaus were opened in 1979 in Peking by AP and UPI as well as the *New York Times, Washington Post, Los Angeles Times,* and *Wall Street Journal.*

Part of the difficulty in reporting Communist societies stems from their definition of news. Under the Communist concept, news is information that serves the interests of the state, that advances its goals and policies. In July 1976, for example, the Chinese saw no particular reason to inform the outside world of a major earthquake in Tangshan, and only unconfirmed rumors filtered through the Bamboo Curtain. Not until early 1977 did the story come out and the outside world learn that rescue workers estimated about 750,000 people were killed or injured in what was perhaps the worst natural disaster of the twentieth century. (The Chinese government itself did not officially acknowledge the loss of life until November 22, 1979, when a small item appeared in the Communist party paper, the *People's Daily*, admitting to 242,000 killed and 164,000 injured). Aircraft crashes and train wrecks are not reported quickly and fully, as they are in the West. So, despite the pervasive international news system, major stories can still go unreported in countries living with the Communist concept.

In addition to TASS, which has personnel in 94 countries and exchange agreements with 40 news agencies, *Pravda*, *Izvestia*, and Novosti (the feature news agency) maintain correspondents abroad. But the Soviet foreign correspondent, because of diplomatic status and immunity is essentially an emissary of the Soviet Union, tends to stress official views in reporting from other lands. News gathering is more akin to intelligence gathering— sending back information of use and interest to officialdom rather than to the average reader. The Soviet media are integrated, planned, and used in a way that the older authoritarian press almost never was. Under traditional authoritarianism, the media were merely controlled; the Soviet media serve the state just as the navy and the railroads do.

Revolutionary Concept

Lenin himself provided some ideology and rationale for another and more ephemeral view, the Revolutionary concept. Simply stated, this is the concept of illegal and subversive mass communications utilizing the press and broadcasting to overthrow a government or wrest control from alien rulers. Lenin in his famous pamphlet, "What is to be Done?" written in exile before the 1917 Revolution, proposed that the revolutionaries establish a nationwide, legal newspaper inside czarist Russia. Such a paper could obviously not advocate revolutionary goals, but its distribution system could be an excellent mechanism for a political machine. The paper, Lenin postulated, would be a cover for a farflung revolutionary organization and a means of communication between followers, a way to keep them in touch. The early *Pravda*, although it was not a legal paper (and which was edited by Stalin at one time), was published outside czarist Russia, and smuggled copies were widely distributed—a fine example of the Revolutionary concept.

The revolutionary press is a press of people who believe strongly that the government they live under does not serve their interests and should be overthrown. They owe the government no loyalty. Pure examples are difficult to find, but one surely was the underground press in Nazi-occupied France during World War II. The editors and journalists of the *Editions Minuit* literally risked their lives to put out their papers and pamphlets. Many other publications called "underground newspapers," such as those that flourished in America during the antiwar protests in the late 1960s, were not truly revolutionary because they were generally tolerated by authorities and the risks of publishing were not great; some editors were harassed, but none were shot by firing squads.

Better contemporary examples of the Revolutionary concept are the *samizdat* ("self-publishing" in Russian), the clandestinely typed and mimeographed copies of books, political tracts, and the like that are passed at great risk from hand to hand among dissidents inside the Soviet Union. Often such publications are merely expressing grievances or petitioning for civil rights, but to authoritarian regimes such expression is clearly revolutionary and subversive.

The history of the anticolonialist movement in the Third World is replete with examples of the Revolutionary concept. Throughout the British Empire, especially in West Africa, political dissidents published small newspapers, often handwritten, that first expressed grievances against the British rulers, then encouraged nationalism, and finally advocated political independence. Aspiring political leaders such as Azikiwe, Awolowo, Nkrumah, Kaunda, and Kenyatta were editors of these small political papers that informed and helped organize the budding political parties and nationalist movements.[5] British authorities were surprisingly tolerant, even though they disapproved of and often acted against the publications and their editors. Much in the Anglo-American tradition supported these papers, and the editors claimed the rights of British journalists. Had not Thomas Paine used political pamphlets to help run the British out of the American Colonies? Had not Thomas Jefferson (and his words were echoed later by Supreme Court Justice William O. Douglas) said the people have a right to revolution, including the right to subsequent revolutions if they proved necessary?

In the postindependence years, radio broadcasting has become a valuable tool of revolutionary groups seeking to overthrow the fragile governments of the Third World. Black Africa has been plagued with numerous coups d'etat, and during times of acute political crisis, radio broadcasting has often played a significant role as the primary medium of mass communication in most nations. Rebels have recognized the importance of controlling information at the political center of power. Hence, insurgents often seize the radio station before heading for the presidential palace. Military struggles during a coup attempt often occur outside the broadcast station, because if rebels can announce over the radio that a coup has been accomplished (even while the issue is still in doubt), it helps accomplish the desired end.[6]

More recently, two other communication inventions—the Xerox machine and the cassette—have proved valuable in revolutionary efforts. In Iran, the revolution of the Ayatollah Khomeini was the first cassette revolution. Thousands of cassette recordings of the Ayatollah's speeches propagating his revolutionary ideas were played in the mosques, which were ignored by the secret police. Moreover, these little portable instruments could reach millions while circumventing the government-controlled press, radio, and television. At the same time, when revolutionary "night letters" and pamphlets arrived mysteriously at offices in Teheran, sypathetic secretaries made many photocopies, quickly and more secretly than possible with a printing press. Anthony Sampson says that "the period of television and radio monopolies may prove a passing phase, as we find ourselves in a much more open field of communications, with cassettes and copied documents taking the place of the books and pamphlets that undermined 18th century governments." He suggested an epitaph for the Shah's regime: "He forgot the cassette."[7]

Even though television and radio—more controllable than the printing press—can give autocratic governments a monopoly of news and propaganda, the Revolutionary concept still can be fostered in divided societies by innovations in more personal and decentralized communication methods.

Developmental Concept

By its very nature, the Revolutionary concept usually is a short-term affair; the successful subversive use of mass communication to topple a despised regime is self-limiting. Once goals are achieved, the gains must be consolidated, and then usually the Authoritarian or Communist concept takes over. But in recent years a variation on the Authoritarian—the Developmental concept—has been emerging in impoverished nations throughout the Third World.

The Developmental concept is an amorphous and curious mixture of ideas, rhetoric, influences, and grievances. As yet, the concept is not clearly defined. There are aspects straight out of Lenin and the Communist concept of the press. Perhaps of greater importance are the influences of Western social scientists who have posited a major role for mass communication in the process of nation-building in newly independent countries. American academics such as Wilbur Schramm, Daniel Lerner, and Lucian Pye, all libertarians at heart, have shown how the communication process is central to the achievement of national integration and economic development; in doing so they have unintentionally provided a rationale for autocratic press controls.

Other more radical academics such as Dallas Smythe of Canada, Kaarle Nordenstreng of Finland, and Herbert Schiller of the United States have echoed Marxist views and added a strong touch of anti-Americanism to the concept. For the concept is to some extent a critique of and reaction against the West and its transnational media. It also reflects the frustrations and anger of poor and impotent nations of the Third World. A major international body, the United Nations Educational, Scientific and Cultural Organization (UNESCO), has provided during the 1970s a forum and soundingboard for the expression of the Developmental concept.

Generally, the concept holds that:

• All the instruments of mass communication—newspapers, radio, television, motion pictures, various information services— must be mobilized by the central government to aid in the great tasks of nation-building: fighting illiteracy and poverty, building a political consciousness, assisting in economic development. Implicit here is the social responsibility view that the government must step in and provide adequate media service when the private sector is unable to do so.

• The media therefore should support authority, not challenge it. There is no place for dissent or criticism, in part because the alternative to the ruling government would be chaos, it is argued.

• Information (or truth) thus becomes the property of the state; the flow of power (and truth) between the governors and the governed works from the top down as in traditional authoritarianism. Information or news is a scarce national resource; it must be utilized to further the national goals.

• Implied but not often articulated is the view that individual rights of expression and other civil liberties are somewhat irrelevant in the face of the overwhelming problems of poverty, disease, illiteracy, and ethnicity that face a majority of these nations.

• This concept of a guided press further implies that in international news, each nation has a sovereign right to control foreign journalists and the flow of news back and forth across its borders.

Some critics say that central to the Developmental concept is the rejection of the Western view. As British journalist

Rosemary Righter argues, there is a growing feeling that the Western model of the press is undesirable in itself. Instead of backing diversity and free flow, the mass media must adopt a didactic, even ideological, role of explaining to the people their part in forging a new social order.[8]

In fact, one of the catch phrases of the concept is that the world needs a New World Information Order to redress these imbalances.

Western news media are attacked on several scores.

To begin with, some critics say the Western international media are too monopolistic and powerful—they penetrate too widely and effectively. The world news agencies—AP, UPI, Reuters, and AFP—are particular targets; they are charged with creating a clear imbalance in the flow of information, which favors the affluent North.

Furthermore, Western media represent an alien viewpoint, which they impose on nations trying to build independent modern identities. Traditional cultures, it is charged, have been threatened by the inundation of news and mass culture—television programs, pop music, movies, etc.—principally from America and Britain. Such domination amounts to cultural aggression.

Western media, critics insist, lack both the accuracy and objectivity on which they have based their claims for preeminence.

Finally, a few proponents of the Developmental concept charge that the Western media are part of an international conspiracy by which the economic and political interests of the capitalist nations are using global mass communication to dominate, even subjugate, the Third World.

The Developmental concept is a view of mass communication from the many nations of the Third World where most people are colored, poor, ill-nourished, and illiterate, and it reflects resentments against the West where people are mainly Caucasians, (except in Japan), affluent, and literate. The concept is directly related to what many feel is the major problem facing the world today: the widening gap between rich and poor nations. The same nations that decry the trade and GNP imbalances between North and South also excoriate the Western news media.

Righter, of the *Sunday Times* of London, whose book *Whose*

News? is an excellent summary of the controversy, believes there is an organized campaign under way—through supranational agencies like UNESCO, in intergovernmental groupings, and in a number of academic and quasi-political institutions—to give the concept of a guided press international respectability.[9]

In the growing confrontation between the Western and Developmental concepts several qualifications are in order. Third World advocacy of a guided media system comes mainly from political leaders and government representatives. Some journalists support this, but many others throughout the Third World—in India, Nigeria, the Philippines, Kenya, Pakistan, and other countries—advocate and try to practice, often under great difficulty, journalism that is independent of state control. Some perceive the Developmental concept as only a temporary and transitional condition pending achievement of a more stable and participant society. In numerous countries where government-controlled media are advocated by unelected leaders and spokesmen in UNESCO, there are journalists, lawyers, and academics who support the values of independent journalism and the free flow of information. And, curiously, government spokesmen in many countries with government-controlled media insist their press and broadcasting are much freer and more open than they actually are.

The controversy engendered by these conflicting concepts of mass communication—between the Western and the Developmental, with its strong overtones of authoritarianism—has heightened in rancor and severity in recent years and shows little sign of abating. There are legitimate arguments on both sides of this political and ideological confrontation, each reflecting differing social, political, and cultural traditions that are difficult to reconcile. As the world becomes smaller, the conflicts over how news and information are to be controlled become ever more serious.

These five concepts of the press may be useful in explaining some of the divergent perceptions of the nature of news and how it should be disseminated. But the problems surrounding the gathering and delivery of international news are more complex and varied than can be neatly catagorized to fit into set classifications.

TABLE 5.1. FIVE CONCEPTS OF THE WORLD'S MEDIA

Type	Control of Media	Information Policy	Representative Countries
Authoritarian	Public and private, subordinate to the state.	Media can operate if there is no criticism of regime or dissent. Implied or actual censorship.	Early European countries. Modern dictatorships in Latin America and elsewhere.
Western (libertarian and social responsibility)	Private ownership of press. Private or public broadcasting systems.	Emphasis on freedom from restraints on news and programming. Press free to criticize government, yet obligated to perform responsibly.	United States, Britain, Western Europe, Japan.
Communist	Media integrated into Communist party and government. No private ownership of media.	Emphasis on transmitting official views and policies; mobilizing support. Consensus valued.	Soviet Union and Communist nations of East Europe, China.
Revolutionary	Illegal or subversive media, uncontrolled by government.	Underground media, often from outside country, seeking to overthrow a government.	Underground media in wartime occupations. Colonial press in parts of Africa, India.
Developmental	Government and/or party controls and directs all media.	Mobilization of media to serve national goals of economic development; political integration; and campaign against poverty, disease, and illiteracy.	Nonindustrialized, non-Communist nations of the Third World.

Notes

1. For this analysis, the author owes a debt to that influential book by Fred Siebert, Theodore Peterson, and Wilbur Schramm, *Four Theories of the Press* (Urbana: University of Illinois Press, 1956). For the purposes of this transnational comparison of press systems, the Libertarian and Social Responsibility theories are both included within the Western concept.
2. Ibid., p. 36.
3. Associated Press v. United States, 52 F. Supp. 362, 372 (1943).
4. Ithiel de Sola Pool. "The Mass Media and Politics in the Modernization Process," in *Communications and Political Development*, ed. Lucian Pye (Princeton, N.J.: Princeton University Press, 1963), pp. 230 ff.
5. E. Lloyd Murphy, "Nationalism and the Press in British West Africa" (Masters thesis, University of Wisconsin-Madison, 1967).
6. William Hachten, "Broadcasting and Political Crisis," in *Broadcasting in Africa: A Continental Survey of Radio and Television*, ed. Sydney Head (Philadelphia: Temple University Press, 1974), pp. 395–98.
7. Anthony Sampson, "Rebel Poli-Techs," *New York Times*, May 6, 1979, opposite editorial page.
8. Rosemary Righter, *Whose News? Politics, the Press and the Third World* (New York: Times Books, 1979), pp. 14–15.
9. Ibid., p. 21.

6

WESTERN PERSPECTIVE
ON WORLD NEWS

> THE cause of the decline and fall of the Roman
> Empire lay in the fact that there were no
> newspapers of the day. Because there were no
> newspapers, there was no way by which the
> dwellers in the far-flung nation and the empire
> could find out what was going on at the
> center.
>
> —H. G. WELLS

THE Nigerian press spokesman smiled at the roomful of reporters, paused dramatically, and said: "Gentlemen, I've got some good news for you today. We are lifting press censorship."

In the commotion that followed, one newsman was heard to shout: "Can we report that?"

"Unfortunately not," replied the spokesman. "You see, we never really said publicly that we were imposing press censorship. Therefore, we can hardly announce today that we are lifting it."[1]

Often when two or more foreign correspondents gather to relax, they exchange stories like this one that reflect the frustrations, the humor, and the ironies of what must be among the most demanding jobs in journalism. And there is no question that transnational news gathering is an exacting occupation for the professional newsmen and women of the Western nations who put together the various stories, reports, rumors, and educated guesses that make up the daily international news file. To them, theirs is a costly, difficult, imperfect, dangerous, and badly misunderstood enterprise. They understand its shortcomings and problems far better, they believe, than their politically motivated non-Western critics. It is, they will point out, the only effective news-gathering system the world has; no viable alternatives exist or are likely to be developed soon.

In a real sense, the world's ability to know the news about itself depends on what gets into the news flow in the 15 or 20 open societies with highly developed media systems. Once an important story appears in New York, London, Paris, Stockholm, or Tokyo, it immediately starts flowing through the arteries of the world's news system and will be widely reported elsewhere—but not everywhere and certainly not every story. For the majority of non-Western governments act as gatekeepers, screening news in and out of their nations. These political controls, as well as poverty and illiteracy, deprive the great majority of the world's peoples of even the barest outline of major current events.

To the few thousand foreign correspondents, the world's nations are strung out on a continuum from "free" or open at one end to "not free" or closed at the other end. To illustrate, the Associated Press has little difficulty gathering news in open Sweden, since several newspapers there take AP services and share their own news and photos with the agency. In addition, AP correspondents can use other Swedish media as sources and can develop their own stories or easily gain access to public officials.

Morocco, as an example of a partly free country, offers a different challenge. AP has no clients in Morocco, whose local media are subject to official controls, and the agency cannot economically justify maintaining a full-time correspondent in Rabat. So AP covers Morocco by using a local stringer (a part-timer who is paid for what is used) who works for a Rabat paper, culling the French media from Paris, and periodically sending a staff correspondent to Morocco to do background stories.

At the not-free end of the continuum are a few countries such as Albania and Guinea, which for years have barred all foreign journalists and news agencies. When something important happens in Tirana or Conakry, AP and the world usually find out about it belatedly from a government-controlled radio broadcast monitored abroad or from travelers or diplomats coming out of the country.

A foreign correspondent defines a country as free or not free according to how much difficulty he or she has in reporting events from that country. This may sound narrow and self-serving, but it has validity; the freedom of access that a foreign reporter has is usually directly related to the amount of independence and access enjoyed by local journalists themselves. If local journalists are harassed and/or controlled by a particular government, so very likely will be the foreign journalists. Throughout the unstable and volatile Third World, some nations swing back and forth. For example, under Indira Gandhi, India, the world's largest democracy, went through a not-free period when the local press was controlled and foreign correspondents were forced to leave or were subjected to censorship. Later, in the period when she was out of office, news access opened again, and the country regained the free press for which India had been noted.

Despite the widespread availability of impressive gadgets and hardware—comsats, telex, video display terminals, computers—collecting news throughout the world is still an erratic and imperfect process. Some significant events are either not reported or reported long after the fact. Certain areas of the world, such as central Africa, rarely get into the world news flow. Datelines from such capitals as Niamey, Bamako, Khartoum, Ouagadougou, Lomé, Freetown, Conakry, Bangui, Yaoundé, Nouakchott, or Brazzaville rarely appear in Western newspapers unless the stories concern violent conflict or a coup d'etat.

Central to this situation are disagreements between professional journalists and government officials over the nature of news. To the journalist, news is the first fragmentary and incomplete report of a significant event or happening that editors back home think will be of interest or importance to their readers or listeners. To government officials, news is information that reflects well on their nation (and hence themselves) and serves their country's general interests and goals. Yet those same leaders want to know all that is happening elsewhere that affects their interests and country. Keith Fuller, the head of AP, put it well: "News is what a government official wants to read, propaganda is what the official wants the world to read about him and his country."

Politicians and government leaders in every nation along the free to not-free continuum attempt to manage or manipulate the news so that it favors their causes, their programs.

Too Few Correspondents

"What is commonly referred to as the world flow of information," former AP foreign correspondent Mort Rosenblum wrote, "is more a series of trickles and spurts. News is moved across borders by a surprisingly thin network of correspondents. . . . The smaller countries are squeezed into rapid trips during lulls between major stories in the larger countries." Rosenblum quoted a comment from a Latin American academic that "news breaks in South America along the direct lines of the Braniff route."[2]

The fact is that there are far too few journalists stationed overseas. Ralph Kliesch of Ohio University found a decline in the number of Americans abroad during the early 1970s. In 1969, there were 563 U.S. correspondents abroad. This dropped to 524 in 1972 and to 435 in 1975, a 23 percent decrease in six years. And the number of full-time journalists of other nationalities working for U.S. media fell from 366 to 247.[3]

The same trend is evident in Britain. A Royal Commission determined that between 1965 and 1976, only 3 of 10 national newspapers had increased their foreign staffs; only 1 of those 3 had not cut back in the lean years since 1974. In just over 10 years, the *Times* had dropped from 25 to 18 its reporters abroad, the *Daily Telegraph*, from 30 to 13.

Rising costs and inflation have made maintenance of a staffer overseas quite expensive. Estimates range from $80,000 to $150,000 for keeping one full-time correspondent abroad for one year; it is not surprising, therefore, that so many media rely on the news agencies for foreign news.

A 1979 State Department study concluded that the number of foreign correspondents seems to be stabilizing and may even have increased slightly.[4] AP's foreign news corps grew from 65 full-time U.S. newspersons in 1975 to 81 in 1979. United Press International's foreign staff remained stable at 80. Both the

Chicago Tribune and Knight-Ridder papers were increasing their foreign staffs, and in 1979, the *New York Times, Washington Post, Los Angeles Times,* and *Wall Street Journal* each installed a correspondent in Peking to join AP and UPI, which had 2 reporters each there.

The *New York Times* had 34 correspondents abroad in 1978, half of what it had overseas in the 1950s. Although the paper probably covers the world better than any daily, it is ironic that there are more reporters in its Washington Bureau than in the rest of the world. Still, it has the largest number of foreign correspondents of any of the major U.S. newspapers committed to overseas coverage. The *Los Angeles Times,* which enlarged its foreign staff in the 1970s, keeps 18 reporters abroad. The *Washington Post* also expanded its foreign coverage during the same period. At the end of the decade, it was devoting about 10 news columns or about 10,000 words a day to foreign news. Most of this was supplied by 16 staff correspondents and 20 active overseas stringers and handled by a foreign desk of 11 specialists on foreign affairs. The excellent foreign coverage in the *Post* costs the paper about $3,500,000 annually.[5]

Among the few other U.S. papers committed to foreign coverage are the *Wall Street Journal* with a dozen correspondents abroad in 1979, the *Christian Science Monitor* with eight, and the *Baltimore Sun* with six. Almost all the other 1,750 U.S. dailies relied on the news agencies and syndicates for their foreign news.

Time and *Newsweek* each maintain 20 to 25 staffers abroad, somewhat below their totals of earlier times. The three major television networks each have 14 to 20 correspondents overseas. CBS, during the mid-1970s, had 75 correspondents to cover the United States and only 14 for the rest of the world. NBC, with about 55 national correspondents, had full-time correspondents and crews in only 20 foreign capitals from which they covered the whole of Africa, Asia, Europe, and South America.

Not only are correspondents few in number, they are unequally distributed as well. Kliesch found that 54 percent of Americans and 51 percent of all correspondents abroad were stationed in 19 European countries. Of these, only 7 to 8 percent were in 3 East European nations, mainly the USSR. Kliesch discovered only token representation in Africa, with full-time correspondents in only 4 countries: Kenya (with half the entire African total), Nigeria, Ethiopia, and South Africa. Since Kliesch's study, both Nigeria and Ethiopia have barred U.S. reporters.

In 1981, about 85 foreign correspondents were based in Johannesburg, mainly because it was then a hub for air travel and comsat transmission for southern Africa, where much news was breaking in several neighboring countries. For when a major international story breaks, almost a herd instinct begins operating that brings numerous reporters and cameramen flying to the scene. In December 1979, during the height of the Iranian crisis when 53 Americans were held as hostages, more than 300 Western newsmen and women, some 100 of them Americans, were working in Teheran. Such "parachute journalism" does not always provide informed coverage, because many of these reporters have no previous knowledge of or experience in the country about which they are reporting.

New York and Washington, D.C., are world news centers, and Hamid Mowlana counted 835 foreign correspondents in the United States representing 550 publications, broadcasting corporations, and news agencies from 73 countries (not one of which was a black African state). Most represented with correspondents in the United States were Britain (102), West Germany (90), Japan (82), France (72), Italy (56), and Canada (43).[6]

Such statistics reflect the reality that most world news originates in the major cities of New York, Washington, D.C., London, Paris, Tokyo, Hong Kong, Bonn, Rome, and Moscow, and foreign correspondents tend to congregate in such places.

Quantity and Quality of News

For American readers at least, serious questions have been raised about the quantity and quality of the foreign news they receive. AP and UPI editors have long maintained that their services gather ample amounts of foreign news but that their newspaper and broadcast clients do not use very much of it. The clients, in turn, say that their readers and viewers are not interested. Critics say that Americans are uninformed about the world because their news media report so little about it.

At times, some segments of the American press deliberately cut back the space allotted for foreign news. In 1975, Martin Arnold of the *New York Times* found a trend developing on many newspapers around the country: hit heavily on local news and "people" and "service" articles; deemphasize national and foreign news.[7] In Arnold's view, this was partly a reaction to apparent reader weariness after the trauma of Watergate and the Vietnam War and may also have reflected a new isolationism and apathy toward affairs not of direct concern to the individual.

Certainly there is truth in the generalization that the majority of Americans, with access to the world's most pervasive media, are ill formed on world affairs. Foreigners traveling in the American heartland are uniformly impressed by the lack of world news in the local media and the ignorance shown by most Americans about the outside world. By contrast, the average West German, Dane, Swiss, or Israeli knows more global news because his or her media carries more.

Part of the problem is that Americans, like the Russians and Chinese, have a continental outlook, living as they do in the midst of a vast land mass that encourages a self-centered, isolationist view of the world. With two friendly neighbors and protected by two oceans, Americans are slow to realize their dependence on others.

Thus Americans' interest in foreign news has its ups and downs. During the Vietnam War, there was much concern about what was happening in Southeast Asia, but not about Latin America or Africa. After Vietnam, there was a pulling back from foreign concerns as the nation became enthralled by Watergate and its aftermath.

But after the rapid increase in the price of foreign oil, the Iranian crisis, and the Soviet incursion into Afghanistan, the average American's interest in foreign news clearly increased. In addition, there is some evidence that the public is more interested in foreign news than editors believe. A 1978 Louis Harris poll on public attitudes toward news found that "those who work in the media (editors, news directors, and reporters) feel that only 5 percent of the public are greatly interested in international news. A much higher 41 percent of the public express deep interest in world affairs being covered in the news media."[8]

In January 1980, a consensus of some 700 readers agreed

with UPI editors on the top 10 stories of the 1970s, and most of those stories had strong international orientation. The decade's top 10 stories were:

1. Richard Nixon resigns as president.
2. The energy crisis: Arab oil embargoes, search for alternatives.
3. Vietnam War ends with Communist victory.
4. The economy: U.S. and world-wide inflation, dollar's decline.
5. The Middle East: War, Egyptian-Israeli peace treaty.
6. Guyana massacre and suicides.
7. U.S. and China normalize relations.
8. Nuclear accident at Three Mile Island.
9. Space exploration: Apollo, Skylab, Soyuz, Mars probe.
10. Shah ousted in Iran; Islamic republic established.[9]

There is perhaps a growing recognition that the term "foreign news" is a misnomer and that in this interdependent world we are potentially affected by any event almost anywhere. Americans waiting in gas lines or watching the devaluation of the dollar and resulting inflation are becoming more knowledgeable about world economic realities.

Performance Criticized

The use of foreign news in the U.S. media raises two questions: Are news media fulfilling their obligation of providing essential information so their readers can make sound judgments on foreign and national affairs? Are media helping instead to make Americans more provincial at a time when the world is getting smaller?

A study based on a series of surveys of journalists and newspapers found that American newspapers generally are lax in their coverage of international news. Researchers Lester Markel and Audrey March concluded that the majority printed little more than the bare essentials, not enough to provide any clear view of what is going on in the rest of the world.[10]

The surveys determined that news space given to reporting of foreign news totaled 17 percent of the whole news allotment; however, this figure was misleading, the researchers pointed out, since it included trivia, features, and human interest stories, which if deducted would leave about 10 percent.

"As for quality, there is often a lack of expertness, due to the fact that correspondents are often shifted in order to get a fresh point of view and so do not have the feel of the country that a good dispatch reflects. Interpretation of international news is minimal and in some newspapers, nonexistent. Instead of interpretation, one is likely to find opinion in the guise of background."[11]

Markel and March also undertook a week-long look at foreign news on the nightly television network news broadcasts. The amount of foreign news was found to be exceedingly low on all three networks; interpretation was virtually absent; objectivity, difficult to measure on brief stories, was rated adequate.

The indictment concludes:

Critics of the newspapers and television news broadcasts charge that they fail to supply the essential facts accurately or in perspective; that they barrage the public with a welter of unrelated news stories; that they fail to separate the significant from the trivial; and, much too often, neglect the minority viewpoint. In general, the view was expressed that the media fail to show that international news is relevant to the lives of readers and viewers at a time when actions by the federal government and events in foreign countries may profoundly affect American lives.[12]

Michael J. Arlen, the *New Yorker*'s perceptive television critic, believes that foreign news as a broadcast commodity has been in a steady decline in recent years to such an extent that "it now often seems to be thrown into a network's regular news productions as a kind of afterthought."[13] Even though CBS and NBC claim that the foreign news content of their major news shows averages from 20 to 25 percent, this total, Arlen feels, is actually reached by two narrow types of reporting: semiofficial accounts of the overseas travels and meetings of our presidents and secretaries of state and a largely reflexive, military-oriented coverage of combat situations. "Ongoing interpretive coverage of the world as a whole by U.S. broadcast journalism seems right now to be at a minimum and, despite the profitability of the three networks, shows no signs of becoming more ambitious."[14]

Further, television tends to concentrate for days running on the "big story," such as the U.S. hostages in Iran or the continuing Arab-Israeli crisis, and neglect significant events elsewhere. Perhaps this is inevitable in a "headline service," as

Walter Cronkite has called television news, but it does not help to provide a public, which relies on television as its major source of news, with a fully rounded picture of the world.

There is no doubting, however, the tremendous capacity of television news to focus world attention on some foreign event. The Vietnamese boat people, for instance, or the starving Cambodians had been suffering and enduring hardships for many months, but it was not until the dramatic color television coverage of their plight appeared on the news night after night that the world was galvanized into relief action. To paraphrase a propaganda maxim, the color television report of an event may be as important as the event itself. And the obverse is true as well: an unreported event will have little impact.

For it is inevitable that much of what happens in the world will go unnoted. Wherever he or she may be, the average person does not have the time or interest to follow all the news from everywhere. As one editor asked, "Who wants to read about Zaire if there is nothing going on there?" Gerald Long of Reuters explained more fully: "The prevalent school of journalism throughout the world is a journalism of exception. In other words, you don't report that everything is fine in Pakistan. You report that there has been an air crash."[15]

Hostility to Western Journalists

The journalism of exception—reporting the coup d'etat, the train wreck, the drought—is at the root of the increasing hostility and antagonism toward Western reporting.

Henry Kamm of the *New York Times* believes that the foreign correspondent is becoming a casualty of the self-assertion of the Third World toward the West. "Demonstrating suspicion toward correspondents and reducing their access to sources of news, much of the Third World is gradually joining the Communist nations in closing itself off from critical inquiry," he wrote.[16]

The field of activity of the Western press is being narrowed increasingly by both formal and informal methods. Former AP correspondent Mort Rosenblum categorized four forms that such methods can take.

The "Blackout" approach, which seems to be gaining popularity, takes the view that no news at all is better than critical or unflattering reports abroad, so reporters are kept out. "Reluctant Coverage" means that reporters are permitted in, but access to news sources or officials is severely limited. The Soviet Union, China, and Eastern European countries are examples. The "Subtle Squeeze" occurs in countries that appear to permit open coverage but actually apply indirect restraints on particular stories. Sometimes correspondents are censored by excessive hospitality that keeps them occupied at some distance from a potentially embarrassing story. The fourth method is "Friendly Persuasion," wherein reporters are not restricted, but efforts are made to influence them in a positive way. American officials have been known to use this method, typified by the press junket— taking reporters to the scene of a news story in hopes they will report favorably on it. Much of what is termed "enlightened public relations" falls within this category.[17]

Reluctant Coverage can often be as effective as the Blackout approach in preventing reportage. On a visit to Tanzania, Henry Kamm was told by a government information official that he should have submitted his precise program in writing long before arrival so that a special government committee could rule on his requests. Because he had not done so, Kamm was told he could see no government official and must not leave the capital at the risk of arrest. The only official help he received for a story on Tanzanian development was a collection of speeches of President Julius Nyerere, the most recent, three years old.[18]

David Lamb of the *Los Angeles Times* agrees that the doors are closing to the Western press. "Across the continent," he wrote of Africa, "news management is becoming tighter, restrictions on journalists more severe and access to countries more limited. More than a quarter of Black Africa's 44 governments ban foreign correspondents or admit them infrequently and under such controlled conditions that news, in effect, is managed or blacked out. Others admit journalists only for self-serving group tours, then send them on their way.

"Increasingly, Africa views foreign correspondents as a nuisance. They distort the news, governments argue, by dwelling on the negative and the sensational—or, at least, by raising issues that are best ignored in the interests of a developing nation."[19]

A major point of contention is that most developing nations believe the press should serve their national aims, while the Western press sees itself as a critical appraiser. This is a basic difference between the Western and Developmental concepts of the press.

A few recent examples:

• Zaire expelled a dozen journalists over what it considered unfavorable reporting on the Shaba Province War.

• In Malawi, during the late 1970s, no foreign correspondent had been granted entry for at least three years. UPI's stringer was jailed for three months, then expelled.

• Many reporters cover individual countries by proxy. Idi Amin's Uganda was covered by monitoring Radio Uganda and interviewing diplomats and refugees. Ghana, Guinea, Guinea Bissau, Benin, Equatorial Guinea, and Angola have also been covered from afar because they denied access to Western correspondents.

Nigeria, the most important and populous nation in Africa and a major oil producer, provides a significant case history. In March 1977, John Darnton, the *New York Times* correspondent for western Africa, was arrested and jailed in Lagos and then expelled the following day. He was taken into custody by four security men, his office and home were searched, and he was detained and interrogated for eight hours. He was stripped of his clothing and kept in a tiny, barren cell. Released later, he and his family were escorted to the airport for a plane to Kenya.

Soon afterward, AP and Voice of America closed their Lagos offices, concluding it was impossible to work there. UPI did not have a Nigerian bureau either. Earlier, in 1976, Nigeria had thrown out the resident Reuters reporter by putting him, his wife, and eight-year-old daughter in a dugout canoe headed for Benin. Agence France Presse had the only Western correspondent in Nigeria, and he rarely filed. The Nigerian government, once so open to Western journalists, obviously preferred this kind of self-imposed isolation from the Western news flow.

In April 1979, AP and the News Agency of Nigeria (NAN) signed an agreement under which AP will provide its world news report to NAN and NAN will provide its national news service to AP. Inasmuch as NAN is an official agency, AP will receive only such news as the Nigerian government wants the world to know about Nigeria.

This exclusion of the Western press is not confined to Africa. In 1976, the Philippines refused to allow Arnold Zeitlin, an AP correspondent based in Manila, to return to his office from a trip abroad. Officials said he had been "endangering the security and prestige" of the Philippines. In 1975, Peru decided to expel Edith Lederer of AP, giving her a week's notice. Indonesia banned *Newsweek* magazine and its Asian regional editor, Richard Smith, after he wrote an article, "Indonesia's Fading Hopes," describing high-level corruption and suggesting that President Suharto was losing his grip. Thailand expelled Norman Peagram of the *Far East Economic Review* on the grounds that his articles were "detrimental to national security." Another correspondent for that same Hong Kong weekly, Salamat Ali, a Pakistani national, was sentenced on November 29, 1979, to a year of hard labor by a military court in Pakistan for writing an article about secessionist feelings in Baluchistan province.

Physical Danger

Foreign correspondents often risk their lives while working in hostile countries. In 1977, AP reporter Michael Goldsmith was brought handcuffed into the presence of Emperor Jean-Bedel Bokassa I of the Central African Empire. The ruler suddenly clubbed him to the ground, stepped on his glasses, and began kicking him mercilessly. The rest of the emperor's party joined in, and Goldsmith quickly lost consciousness. He awoke in a tiny detention cell, where he spent the next month. Through diplomatic intercession, Goldsmith was finally released and later said, "What happened to me could happen to any correspondent in countries where the ruler is unstable and regards objective reporting as hostile. I'm concerned that this is something that will spread."[20]

Covering civil wars in the Third World is particularly dangerous for Western correspondents. The protracted invasion of Uganda by Tanzanian forces in 1979 was reported mainly from neighboring Kenya because of hostility to foreign journalists from both sides. In the later stages of the conflict that drove Idi Amin from power, two West Germans, Hans Bollinger and Wolfgang Stiens, and two Swedes, Arne Lemberg and Earl Bergman, entering Uganda to report on the war, were murdered by soldiers loyal to Amin.

Most often, such violence against foreign correspondents is reported sometime after the tragedy. But the murders in Nicaragua of Bill Stewart, a television correspondent for ABC, and his interpreter on June 21, 1979, were viewed by millions the same day on the evening television news. While covering the fighting between government troops and Sandinista rebels (both groups had been hostile to American newsmen), Stewart, explaining at a roadblock that he wanted to interview government soldiers, was told to kneel; moments later a soldier walked over and shot him once in the head with a rifle. The whole episode was recorded by an ABC cameraman from a short distance away. This film, which shocked the nation, also disputed the Nicaraguans' first contention that Stewart was killed while trying to flee.

Local journalists as well as foreign correspondents are often caught in the cross fire of political extremism and violence so widespread in the world today. One survey for a 15-month period in 1977–78 found that at least 24 journalists around the world had been murdered and another 36 were either tortured by police or injured in violent attacks by political extremists. Some 20 more were abducted and many of these are still missing and presumed dead.[21] The 1979 record was equally disturbing. The International Press Institute counted 15 journalists who had lost their lives by violence. It also catalogued 13 assaults against reporters and editors, 12 bombings, more than 30 arrests, 28 expulsions, and 25 jailings. Sixty-nine newspapers were banned or suspended somewhere in the world during the year.

In Argentina alone during the mid 1970s, more than 30 journalists were killed, and 119 were imprisoned, placed under house arrest, or forced into exile, according to AP and the Anti-Defamation League. Foreign journalists there have been pressured as well. Juan de Onis of the *New York Times* was called

in by the Foreign Ministry, which expressed displeasure about
his reportage. Journalists from ABC, NBC, Voice of America,
AP, UPI, and the *Wall Street Journal* have been detained and
questioned for writing about relatives of missing persons.

Retaliation by the West

Western news organizations and their governments are
uncertain how to respond to this treatment of their foreign correspondents. When the Soviet Union expelled AP correspondent
George Krimsky from Moscow in 1977, the U.S. government
retaliated by expelling TASS's correspondent in Washington,
D.C. When the Soviets arrested Robert Toth of the *Los Angeles
Times* the same year and accused him of collecting political and
military secrets, both President Carter and the U.S. Senate de-
nounced the Soviet Union's action. More recently, the White
House and State Department called Soviet correspondents in to
check their credentials in an obvious threat of retaliation for the
harassment by court suits of Craig Whitney of the *New York
Times* and Harold Piper of the *Baltimore Sun*.

Yet the U.S. government does not respond in kind to
harassments of correspondents in the Third World. Stanley
Meisler of the *Los Angeles Times* thinks it should. He wrote:

What is needed is a recognition of the seriousness of the problems, a cry
of warning and some tough talk from the U.S. government and other
governments. The Third World is harassing correspondents more and
more. In some areas, a virtual news blackout exists. This should be
unacceptable to democratic Western governments that deal with these
Third World countries. The peoples of these Western societies have the
right to be informed about the countries with which their governments
are signing trade, aid, and political agreements.[22]

On the other hand, some newspersons feel strongly that the
Western press's independence from government is compromised
when governments intervene on behalf of foreign correspondents.
William Sheehan of ABC urged caution, saying that the U.S.
government should not "directly take up the problems that news
gathering organizations have and intercede with other governments. I feel that the First Amendment precludes such action,
that the government's role should neither be in support nor op-

position to the press. . . . It is best that the government not set any agenda to attempt to find solutions in behalf of the American press."[23]

The difficulties and dangers Western correspondents face from hostile, authoritarian governments appear to be getting worse, and a widespread boycott of the Western press in many Third World countries was seen by *Time* magazine as a distinct possibility. Those who believe in retaliation point out that Western newspersons working in authoritarian countries create a unique situation.

Marshall D. Shulman, an expert on the Soviet Union, said:

The relationship between the government and a newsman working out of Moscow and Peking or any centralized authoritarian situation cannot be equated with newsmen working in Western capitals. His housing, his ability to travel, even his access to food shipments from abroad and his fundamental protection is inextricably related to his government. We have to work out new canons to govern the actions of a democratic society when it is dealing with an authoritarian regime.[24]

Shortcomings of the Western System

In summary, it may be useful to list some of the major shortcomings and inadequacies of the Western system of foreign news gathering.

Far too few journalists and facilities are deployed in the right locations to provide adequate world news coverage. Sparsity of local news media in many nations of Africa, Asia, and Latin America compounds the problem.

Obstructions to news flow are significantly constructed in authoritarian countries by such devices as denial of visas to foreign journalists, censorship, lack of access, and harassment. Ten or 15 years ago, most reporters covering the Third World would have said that their major problems were logistic—getting to the story and then getting the story out to the world. More recently, better air travel and telex via comsats have improved communications, but the political barriers to news gathering have increased markedly.

The limitations of news itself mean that many people somewhere are going to be dissatisfied with how the news is reported. For example, a reporter for the *Los Angeles Times* based in Nairobi, Kenya, is writing for readers some 12,000 miles away in California. His or her stories will be chosen and later edited, not according to what East Africans would prefer, but what editors in Los Angeles think their local readers will be interested in knowing. That correspondent in East Africa may regard, say, development in Tanzania to be an important story, but the resulting dispatch may be discarded because the editor in Los Angeles thinks there is not sufficient interest in the subject.

For news, besides being perishable, is relative and subjective as well as fragmentary and incomplete. Take as an illustration the news of a sudden increase in the price of coffee. In Chicago it means that consumers will be paying 35 cents a pound more for ground coffee—and resenting it very much. To readers in Brazil or the Ivory Coast, the price increase means that coffee-producing nations are receiving a well-deserved break at a time when prices of raw materials from poor nations are lagging further and further behind those of manufactured goods from rich nations.

Furthermore, it is true, unfortunately, that ethnicity or racism does directly affect news values at times. The slaughter of 15 white missionaries by guerrillas in Zimbabwe Rhodesia will make large headlines and arouse public indignation in London, while another story about government forces killing 150 black civilians during a raid into Zambia will be buried on an inside page of the newspaper. Africans notice these discrepancies.

Also, Western news media, although relatively independent of their own governments, will tend to report foreign news from the viewpoint of their country's foreign policy concerns. This is not the result of any conspiratorial link between journalists and a state department or a foreign ministry. Rather, the unsurprising fact is that events abroad are of interest to readers in proportion to the ways national concerns are involved. Turmoil in Iran was a major story in the United States because of our heavy use of Iranian oil.

From 1948 until 1972, the years when the United States refused to recognize Communist China, U.S. reporting about mainland China was generally negative. However, after Nixon and Kissinger went to Peking and the United States played the China card, "Communist China" became the "People's Republic of China," and stories about China in the U.S. media became friendlier and more positive.

News, it has been said, is what an experienced editor puts in the newspaper. And editors—even those on the same newspaper —rarely agree about the importance, value, or credibility of any particular story.

The Western practice of the "journalism of exception"— stressing the disasters, the problems, the upheavals—continues to rankle critics of the press everywhere. In America, many feel the media report far too much negative news. But as Daniel Patrick Moynihan has said, "It is the mark of a democracy that its press is filled with bad news. When one comes to a country where the press is filled with good news, one can be pretty sure that the jails are filled with good men."

Colin Legum of the *Observer* of London, on the other hand, deplores "crisis journalism"—the devotion of too many resources and too much effort to reporting the abnormal in home and international affairs. He wrote:

Of course, crises must be dealt with at length and seriously, but too often this type of journalism is carried to the length of under-reporting the "normal" events, and too often, the crises are allowed to drop right out of sight once the "heat" goes out of the story. My special criticism is of the inadequacy of the in-depth reporting of situations in the post-crisis period. Thus, I may be aware that things are going badly wrong in, say, Sierra Leone, but who, ask my colleagues, is interested in Sierra Leone? The first time readers often become aware of a country's problems is when there has been a military coup, bloodshed, or violent change. Only then is there an "appetite" for information; but at this point most papers are usually much more concerned with reporting the actual events than in devoting a lot of space to serious background reporting—I call the "roots of the problem" journalism.[25]

But the emphasis on crisis journalism is only one of a long list of complaints and criticisms of Western news gathering that have been heard in recent years.

Notes

1. Sean Kelly, *Access Denied: The Politics of Press Censorship*, Washington Papers, no. 55, 1978, p. 10.
2. Rosemary Righter, *Whose News? Politics, the Press and the Third World* (New York: Times Books, 1978), p. 70.

 3. Ralph Kliesch, "A Vanishing Species: The American Newsman Abroad," *Overseas Press Club Directory*, 1975, New York, p. 17.
 4. W. F. Gloede, "Some Newspapers Expand Foreign News Bureaus," *Editor & Publisher*, June 2, 1979, p. 11.
 5. Interview by author with Philip Foisie, assistant managing editor of the *Washington Post*, September 14, 1979.
 6. Hamid Mowlana, "Who Covers America?" *Journal of Communication* 25, no. 3 (Summer 1975): 86–91.
 7. Martin Arnold, "Newspaper Trend: Stress Local News, Cut National and Foreign Coverage," *New York Times*, July 8, 1975, p. 18.
 8. Mort Rosenblum, *Coups and Earthquakes: Reporting the World for America* (New York: Harper & Row, 1979), p. 8.
 9. H. L. Stevenson, *UPI Reporter*, January 3, 1980, pp. 1–2.
10. Lester Markel and Audrey March, *Global Challenge to the United States* (Cranbury, N.Y.: Associated University Presses, 1976), pp. 121–23.
11. Ibid.
12. Ibid.
13. Michael J. Arlen, "The Air: The Eyes and Ears of the World," *The New Yorker*, January 6, 1975, pp. 52 ff.
14. Ibid.
15. Righter, *Whose News?* p. 71.
16. Henry Kamm, "Third World Rapidly Turning into a Closed World for the Foreign Correspondent," *New York Times*, January 14, 1976.
17. Rosenblum, *Coups and Earthquakes*, pp. 98 ff.
18. Kamm, "Third World."
19. Dispatch by Lamb for Los Angeles Times Service printed in the *Milwaukee Journal*, October 8, 1977.
20. "Beating the Press," *Newsweek*, August 29, 1977, p. 54.
21. Andrew Kopkind, "Publish and Perish," *More* 8, no. 4 (April 1978): 13.
22. Stanley Meisler, "Covering the Third World (or trying to)," *Columbia Journalism Review*, November/December 1978, p. 38.
23. I. William Hill, "News Execs Testify on Information Policy," *Editor & Publisher*, June 25, 1977, p. 12.
24. Deirdre Carmody, "Press and Its Independence," *New York Times*, February 8, 1979, p. 2.
25. Colin Legum, "Some Problems Confronting a Correspondent Specializing in Reporting Africa," in *Reporting Africa*, ed. Olav Stokke (New York: Africana Publishing, 1971), pp. 203 ff.

7

Third World Views
of News Flow

> The present information order, based as it is
> on a quasi-monopolistic concentration of the
> power to communicate in the hands of a few
> developed nations, is incapable of meeting the
> aspirations of the international community.
>
> —Mustapha Masmoudi of Tunisia

In Freetown, Sierra Leone, a group of women and children stand immobilized in front of a large television monitor outside the state-owned broadcasting company. Several of the women, wearing traditional *temle* and *lapa* of colorfully patterned cloth, are carrying babies in slings on their backs. All are transfixed by an episode of "The Flintstones."

An item in the *Times of India* about a Cambodian refugee camp in Thailand carries a Reuters credit line.

A businessman in the crowd waiting for the opening of the bank in Ouagadougou, Upper Volta, carries a transistor radio blaring Charles Aznavour singing "J'ai Vu Paris."

In Latin America, scholars write books about Donald Duck as a propagandist for sinister capitalistic values with such titles as "How to Read Donald Duck: Mass Communication and Colonialism."

These media snapshots from around the Third World are more than merely vivid and fascinating vignettes that catch the attention of a Western visitor. They are in fact illustrations of the

issues at the heart of the extraordinary controversy over the control of the flow of global news and mass culture, a controversy
that expanded during the 1970s and is still unresolved.

The disagreements and disputes about the matter reflect the
widening chasm between the few affluent industrialized nations
and the many nonindustrialized countries that consider themselves victimized recipients of a one-way flow of communication.
The dispute is political in part and stems from power and economic relationships. On the one hand, the technological and industrial capacity of developed societies includes an awesome
capability to communicate. Underdeveloped and poor nations
have, by comparison, inadequate communication systems and so
become largely passive recipients of the expanding flow of global
communication including, in addition to news, a great deluge of
mass culture—motion pictures, television and radio programs,
recordings, and various publications.

Essentially, this widening breach over international communication results from differences in economic and social structures as well as conflicting concepts of media controls. The
Western model of news gathering and dissemination is largely re-
jected by the Socialist countries and the new autocracies of the
Third World.

As the *Guardian's* Martin Woollacott put it:

The freedom of the Anglo-American press to roam the world, criticizing,
commenting and generally poking its nose into the affairs of most non-
Western societies, is something we have taken for granted since the
end of the Second World War. The obeisance to democratic ideas at
that time elevated the rights of the foreign press into one of the lesser
principles of international life, like diplomatic immunity or airline
agreements. It was a principle subscribed to by all non-Communist
countries, even where the freedom of their domestic press came to be
curtailed. But we are now fast approaching a point where not only is it
honored more in the breach than the observance, but the principle itself
is under direct attack. [1]

The Western approach to news gathering was embodied in
Article 19 of the United Nations' "Universal Declaration of
Human Rights," voted in 1948, that stated in part: "Everyone
has the right to freedom of opinion and expression . . . and to
seek, receive and impart information and ideas through any
medium and regardless of frontiers."

Western journalists claim there must be a "free flow of communication" to accomplish this. Peoples everywhere, it is pointed out, should have access to information, especially information that affects their security, well-being, and destiny; therefore, journalists must have an unimpeded right to collect and distribute news and information.

This view, for a considerable time, was the official position of the United Nations and especially of the United Nations Educational, Scientific and Cultural Organization (UNESCO), which has a special concern for international communication.

But by 1972, the Western concept of free flow was under attack as typified by declarations of both the UNESCO General Conference and the UN General Assembly concerning satellite broadcasting. On November 15, 1972, the UNESCO General Assembly adopted the "Draft Declaration of Guiding Principles on the Use of Satellite Broadcasting." The vote was 55 to 7, with the United States voting against adoption and 22 countries abstaining. The strongest indication of retreat from unqualified support of international free flow was in Article 9, which subscribed to the necessity of prior agreements between nations before direct satellite broadcasting occurs:

"It is necessary that states, taking into account the principle of freedom of information, reach or promote prior agreements concerning direct satellite broadcasting to the population of countries other than the country of origin of transmission."

Within weeks after UNESCO acted, a UN General Assembly vote directed the UN Outer Space Committee to formulate guiding principles governing direct satellite broadcasts. Impetus for the action was the Soviet Union's proposal that any international agreement on satellites should stipulate regulations against broadcasting into sovereign states without permission. The vote for adoption of the UN General Assembly's directive was 101 to 1, the United States alone dissenting.

These international bodies, composed mostly of the recently independent nations of the Third World, have been fashioning a major modification of the principle of free flow by espousing the idea that international communicators must obtain prior consent of the nations into which their journalists and news reports may move. In the Western view, this is but a short step to the

Authoritarian concept that each government has the inherent right to control news moving back and forth across its borders.

Throughout the 1970s, UNESCO has been a leading forum for this debate, which has involved, in addition to UNESCO and diplomatic representatives of all nations, communication scholars and academics and professional journalists and their organizations such as International Press Institute, Inter American Press Association, International Federation of Journalists, and the International Organization of Journalists, a Communist bloc organization. Much has been written and many speeches have been given as the controversy has accelerated with increasing passion and acrimony. U.S. communication scholar Ithiel Pool commented: "One could fill a volume with heated quotations from unhappy nationalists, guilt-ridden Westerners, worried reactionaries, and angry radicals attacking the free flow of information as a Western plot to impose its culture on helpless people."[2] Be that as it may, the controversy is a serious one and it shows no sign of abating.

The dispute is complicated, involving a number of diverse issues. One of the first involved the direct broadcast satellite, the innovation in comsat technology that makes it possible for an individual television set to receive programming from abroad directly from a comsat, bypassing the ground station that heretofore has allowed each nation to screen or censor undesirable material.

However, this debate over the impact of direct satellite broadcasting may be largely academic because, as Pool suggested, it may be technologically possible for a nation to easily control such a "dangerous" innovation. The continuing debate seems to overlook the fact that international radio broadcasters have been beaming their messages of news, propaganda, music, etc. directly into shortwave radio receivers for many years without international agreements or prior consent. The television picture apparently is perceived as being far more dangerous than the radio word.

The concern here is with international news and the criticism of the Western news media; in this, the Third World has not lacked spokesmen for its views.

Mustapha Masmoudi, former secretary of state for information, Tunisia, has emerged as one of the more articulate critics, and his views are widely accepted in the Third World. In a 1978 paper prepared for UNESCO, he set forth his case against the Western news system.

Information in the modern world, Masmoudi said, is characterized by basic imbalances, reflecting the general economic and social imbalances that affect the international community. In the following seven-point complaint, Masmoudi said that in the political sphere, there is:

1. *A flagrant quantitative imbalance between North and South.* "This imbalance is created by the disparity between the volume of news and information emanating from the developed world and intended for the developing countries and the volume of the flow in the opposite direction." Almost 80 percent of the world news flow comes from the major transnational agencies, but these agencies devote too little attention to the Third World, Masmoudi charged.

The Western world news agencies—Associated Press, Reuters, Agence France Presse, and United Press International—are the particular targets because they are virtually the only sources of world news available to the Third World, where three-quarters of the population live. Presently without alternatives, the Third World is dependent on them for news about themselves and their neighbors.

2. *An inequality in information resources.* "The five transnational news agencies (including TASS) monopolize between them the essential share of material and human potential while a third of the developing nations do not yet possess even a single national agency."

3. *A de facto hegemony and a will to dominate.* Masmoudi said, "Such hegemony and domination are evident in the marked indifference of the media in the developed countries, particularly in the West, to the problems, concerns, and aspirations of the developing countries. They are founded on financial, industrial, cultural and technological power and result in most of the developing countries being relegated to the status of mere consumers of information sold as a commodity like any other. They

are exercised above all through the control of the information flow, wrested and wielded by the transnational agencies operating without let or hindrance in most developing countries and based in turn on the control of technology, illustrated by the communications systems satellites, which are wholly dominated by the major international consortia." Masmoudi expresses here the suspicion of technology and the sense of impotence and exploitation felt in many poor nations.

4. *A lack of information on developing countries.* Masmoudi added: "By transmitting to the developing countries only news processed by them, that is, news which they have filtered, cut and distorted, the transnational media impose their own way of seeing the world upon the developing countries. As a result, communities geographically close to each other sometimes learn about each other only via these transnational systems. Moreover, the latter often seek to present these communities—when indeed they show interest in them—in the most unfavorable light, stressing crises, strikes, street demonstrations, putsches, etc., or even holding them up to ridicule."

5. *Survival of the colonial era.* "The present day information system," Masmoudi wrote, "enshrines a form of political, economic and cultural colonialism which is reflected in the often tendentious interpretation of news concerning the developing countries." The Western media, he declared, are selective in what they report, overlooking some things and overstressing other events. "The criteria governing selection are consciously or unconsciously based on the political and economic interests of the transnational system and the countries in which this system is established. The use of labels and persuasive epithets and definitions, chosen with the *intention* of denigrating, should also be stressed." In this view, then, Western media are identified with colonialism and, in the ways they report global news, perhaps pursue conspiratorial goals.

6. *An alienating influence in the economic, social, and cultural spheres.* Masmoudi perceived other sinister forms of hegemony beyond the domination and manipulation of the international news flow. Besides possession of the media through direct investment, "there is another form of control, far more decisive,

namely, the near monopoly on advertising throughout the world exercised by the major advertising agencies, which operate like the media transnationals, and serve the interests of the multinational business corporations which themselves dominate the business world. Moreover, advertising, magazines, and television programmes are today so many instruments of cultural domination and acculturation, transmitting to the developing countries messages which are harmful to their cultures, contrary to their values and detrimental to their development aims and efforts," Masmoudi charged.

7. *Messages ill suited to the area in which they are disseminated.* "Even important news may be deliberately neglected by the major media in favor of other information of interest only to public opinion in the country to which the media in question belong. . . . Their news coverage is designed to meet the national needs of their countries of origin. They also disregard the impact of news beyond their own frontiers," he said.

Then in a statement for which there is widespread sympathy in the Third World, Masmoudi wrote: "The fact cannot therefore be blinked that the present information order, based as it is on a quasi-monopolistic concentration of the power to communicate in the hands of a few developed nations, is incapable of meeting the aspirations of the international community, which stands in great need of a system capable of fostering more satisfactory dialogue, conducted in a spirit of mutual respect and dignity."[3]

Although details may differ, Masmoudi generally represents the series of Third World complaints about the Western news media that have been made repeatedly in recent years:

• The world news agencies monopolize the flow of news.

• Alien and irrelevant values and life styles of the West are imposed on developing societies through a one-way flow of news that amounts to "cultural imperialism."

• News from the Third World is often negative and distorted.

• Existing lines of communication are vertical, running from North to South, and there is too little news from, say, Asia to Africa and vice versa.

• Developing societies cannot afford a free press, and freedom from want must come before freedom of expression. Hence, the media must be recruited to serve the broad national interests of development.

• Developing nations must control not only their own media but also the flow of information in and out of their countries.

Attack on Free Flow

This bill of indictment of the Western media, valid as it may be in some details, is disturbing to Western journalists, who believe that the concept of free flow and the rights of journalists to report the news are directly challenged.

There are two major arguments against free flow: (1) free flow is a reality only for the rich industrialized nations and (2) these nations would use any increased dominance over world communication flow to promote their imperialist aims.

Recent studies, such as those of Tapio Varis of Finland, certainly have documented the obvious: information and mass culture move mainly in one direction—from rich to poor nations, from North to South, from North America and Europe to the great southern tier of Asia, Africa, and Latin America. (There is also a heavy and fairly even flow of communication *between* the industrialized nations.) But in rebuttal a Western journalist could ask: Who ever said a free flow must be an even flow? Information is essential for development, and for many new nations the modern influx of information of all kinds—books, mass communication, scientific and technological know-how, etc.—is unprecedented in world history. An unbalanced flow is certainly better than no flow at all. The very existence of this widely criticized uneven flow has enabled many areas of the world (black Africa, for example) to participate in world affairs and receive essential information long unavailable when they were colonial wards of European nations.

President Urho Kekkonen of Finland has lent support to the anti-Western charges:

At the international level are to be found the ideals of free communications and their actual distorted execution for the rich on the one hand and the poor on the other. Globally the flow of information between the states—not the least the material pumped out by television—

is to a very great extent a one-way unbalanced traffic and in no way possesses the depth and range of which the principles of freedom of speech require.[4]

But a more widely heard (and popular) argument among non-Western nations is that the rich, industrialized nations are using their communication dominance—this "cultural imperialism"—to perpetuate "neocolonialist" conspiracies.

This is essentially an authoritarian argument, one shared by leftist intellectuals, Communist officials, and political leaders of some Third World nations. U.S. scholar Herbert Schiller has been one of the most articulate spokesmen of this view and argues that it is the corporate interests of the powerful communication nations—notably the United States—that dominate international communication and threaten the cultural sovereignty of vulnerable developing nations. He wrote: " . . . free flow of information, much like free trade in an earlier time, strengthens the strong and submerges the weak. In the case of information, the powerful communication states overwhelm the less developed countries with their information and cultural messages."[5]

Because they lack capital and media resources, the poorer nations must rely on the foreign media for world news, television programming, movies, etc., and as a result, Schiller said, the Third World has been unable to defend itself against the "communications onslaught of the West." He equated this situation to the "blood and iron" imperialism of a previous era, except that economics and communications are now the weapons that further the neocolonial expansion of American power in the world. Not only is the media content Western oriented, Schiller argued, the accompanying advertising is designed to further the interests of U.S. and other multinational corporations.

Schiller wrote: "The international community is being inundated by a stream of commercial messages that derive from the marketing requirements of (mostly) American multi-national companies. The structure of national communication systems and the programming they offer are being transferred according to the specifications of international marketeers."[6]

Schiller argues that developing nations are harmed in two ways. First, presentation of alien and incompatible life styles and images is leading to replacement of local and traditional cultures, creating a worldwide cultural homogenization based on Western, materialistic values. Second, the artificial stimulation of a demand for Western products is contributing to a rise in the frustrations of Third World peoples unable to obtain the consumer goods they see promoted in Western media.

The exporting of Western mass culture is considered by many people, including some in Western nations, to be cultural intrusions that properly can be subjected to regulations designed to protect the integrity of local traditions and infant mass communication industries. Most Western nations, in fact, accept the social responsibility view that some regulation, especially of the violent and the obscene, can be justified.

However, many solutions to "cultural imperialism" proposed in UN bodies are disturbing to Western critics because they would go much further and would legitimize censorship per se. The result would be less communication, not more, and peoples living in authoritarian nations would be "protected against dangerous ideas" by being denied the right to choose and select. This is already the case in most closed nations, but UN endorsement would put the stamp of approval on censorship.

To overcome the perceived domination by Western media, Masmoudi and his colleagues argue, the Third World must establish its "right to communicate"—to talk back. This means disestablishing Western communication rights, which are based upon "individualist considerations to the detriment of collective needs." Freedom to communicate should no longer be limited, they say, to those who own or control the media.

To effect change, a series of "musts" was laid down by Masmoudi:

• Third World countries *must* not be shown in an unfavorable light.

• The world media *must* reserve more space and time for news of developing countries.

• News flowing to a country *must* not clash with that nation's cultural and moral values.

• The content, volume, and intensity of flow between developed and developing countries *must* be "free and equitable."

All of this can only be achieved, Masmoudi argued, with a New World Information Order that calls for:

1. regulation of the right to information by preventing abusive use of the right to access of information;
2. definition of appropriate criteria to govern truly objective news selections;
3. regulation of the collection, processing, and transmission of news and data across national frontiers;
4. enforcement through domestic legislation and new supranational agency of a proposed international journalistic code and penalties; and
5. [assurance that the state can] have published a communique rectifying and supplementing the false or incomplete information already disseminated.[7]

Any response to Masmoudi's criticism comes back to the concept of *diversity* in global news communication. Most of the developing world needs more and better news media, especially regional or non-Western news agencies of its own.

For some years now, news agencies intended specifically for the needs of the Third World have been discussed and even tried. Best known is the Non-Aligned News Agencies Pool (NANAP), which dates from the Fourth Non-Aligned Summit in Algiers in 1973. Although about 80 nations are involved, the pool is really led by Yugoslavia and its agency, Tanjug. Participants send items marked "pool" to Tanjug in Belgrade by any means at their disposal and at their own expense. The daily limit is about 500 words. In some cases, Tanjug merely monitors a nation's news service under an exchange agreement and selects and edits items for inclusion in the pool portion of Tanjug's daily transmission. Stories are accepted in any language and translated into English, Spanish, and French and broadcast daily by Tanjug via high-frequency radio teletype (RTT). Anyone with a compatible teletype receiver and printer can receive the transmission. Tanjug officials say their signal is of good quality worldwide except on the western side of the Andes.

However, participation to date in NANAP leaves much to be desired; only 26 nations of 80 are active, and 10 of them contribute 1 percent or less of the items in the pool. By numbers of news items carried, the most active nations in 1979 were

Yugoslavia, 17 percent; Egypt, 12 percent; Iraq, 7 percent; Cuba, Qatar, Sri Lanka, Libya, each 6 percent; Cyprus, 5 percent; India and Morocco, 4 percent. Thus 60 percent of the pool's content was contributed by just 7 countries.

An obvious problem with NANAP is that the news comes from government news agencies. This can create credibility problems within the pool, because one government is often suspicious of the news issued by another government, especially if political differences exist.

Caught between conflicting interests and limited resources, NANAP's operations are constrained by poor communications, lack of trained journalists, and the sheer diversity of countries in the pool. Some regard each other as bitter enemies. So far, NANAP has proved it can be a supplement to, but not a substitute for, the Western news agencies.

Still in the talking stage is another proposal, made by Narinder Aggarwala, an Indian journalist working with the United Nations Development Programme (UNDP), for a Third World News Agency. He postulates a counterflow of world news that will be southern oriented, both in concept as well as perspective. He envisions an independent Third World agency that will be multinational in operations and management and staff but independent of both national governments and national news agencies. An organization of a loose conglomerate of autonomous and regional news agencies would be formed.

Still another proposal has come from Roger Tatarian, former UPI editor and now a journalism teacher, at a 1978 Cairo Conference on the International News Media and the Third World. Tatarian suggested the formation of a Multinational News Pool to fill the gap in reporting by Western news agencies. The pool would concentrate on cultural, economic, and social developments in the Third World, leaving political events and other daily coverage to the existing agencies. Replying to African suspicions that the proposal might be a ploy to undermine the existing NANAP, he said that it would supplement rather than replace the pool and was designed to help increase news coverage in the Third World.

As Tatarian conceptualized it, the news pool would be organized by a 12-member directorate divided among developed and developing nations. The directorate would ask Western agencies and major newspapers to lend experienced reporters for at least one year on full salary to work abroad producing the sort of features that critics claim the Western media miss. Project funds would come from participating countries. Once established, the multinational pool, Tatarian said, would serve as a central clearing house or a natural bridge for other forms of cooperation between First and Third World journalists. The proposal is significant because it represents an effort by a Western journalist to respond to the concerns of non-Western critics.

Unquestionably, alternate news agencies are needed to provide additional sources of information and hence more diversity. But they do face problems, and the Western media's main concern is that other international news agencies and their correspondents would be excluded from member countries once these pools were functioning. Thus a Third World pool would have a virtual monopoly of information to, from, and about the Third World. The need clearly is not for less but more coverage of Africa, Asia, and Latin America and more reporting from more journalists that is reliable, objective, and thorough. This cannot be achieved in a world blighted by restraints, restrictions, and outright controls on journalists.

Nonetheless, newspapers and broadcasting media in Central Africa or Southeast Asia should not have to rely entirely upon a news agency based in London or New York to find out what is happening in their own region. There should be a greater diversity and variety of sources of news for the world's nations to draw upon. For that reason alone the persistent efforts in Africa, Asia, and Latin America to establish regional news agencies and broadcasting exchange agreements should be continued despite the difficulties involved. But because of the realities of politics in the Socialist and Third World countries, these proposals will come from authoritarian governments, and the Western journalist will be suspicious and skeptical of any government involvement in the flow of news.

A *Milwaukee Journal* editorial expressed this concern:

The purpose of these [Third World] agencies is to tell the "truth" about events in underdeveloped countries. If that were the extent of the governments' ambitions, this so-called new source of news should be welcomed. But underlying these efforts is the dark suspicion that these governments intend to make these agencies the exclusive source of news in their countries. In New Delhi, there were calls for retaliation against and punishment of foreign news services and correspondents who these governments claim were "distorting" information. The participating governments, it seems, only want to hear and disseminate one truth— theirs.[8]

For in the Third World, as well as in countries of the Communist commonwealth, there is as yet too little value attached to independent, nongovernmental news gathering activities, especially if those Western news reports seem to be identified with capitalist Western governments.

In Latin America, for example, young radicals are very suspicious of U.S. news media as personified by AP, UPI, *Time,* or *Newsweek.* They are often hostile toward their own newspapers, which seem to speak out only for the vested interests of the landowners, the church, and the military, which oppose needed reforms. These young militants loudly espouse the nationalization of the press so that it can then, as a voice of government, speak for ALL the people (assuming their government is to their liking). Here again is the argument that only the "good" or "right-thinking" press deserves to be allowed to publish. However, the sad lesson of history is that the demise of even right-wing newspapers that serve only as mouthpieces of the privileged minority has meant the demise of what few political liberties existed. Many coups d'etat, revolutions, and military takeovers around the world attest to this. Once lost, individual liberty and free expression are difficult to regain.

Given the worldwide problems of poverty, economic inequality, famine, burgeoning populations, ethnicity, etc. that beset so many nations, radical situations or socialist revolutions may indeed be called for, but they should not be at the cost of freedom and an unimpeded flow of reliable information. For as author and critic Irving Howe wrote: "The central lesson of politics in our century has been that *any* regime that suppresses democratic liberties (including press freedom) has no right, political or moral, to the designation of 'socialism.' "

The major barrier to reliable, unimpeded world news flow comes down, finally, to differences in politics and economics between the few Western democracies and the great majority of nations that are under varying degrees of authoritarian rule, whether Communist, Developmental, or whatever.

Notes

1. Martin Woollacott, "Western News-gathering: Why the Third World Has Reacted," *Journalism Studies Review* 1, no. 1 (June 1976): 12.
2. Ithiel de Sola Pool, "Direct Broadcast Satellites and the Integrity of National Cultures," *Control of the Direct Broadcast Satellite: Values in Conflict* (Palo Alto, Calif.: Aspen Institute, 1974), pp. 27–35, 45–56.
3. Mustapha Masmoudi, "The New World Information Order" (Paper presented and discussed at the third session of the International Commission for the Study of Communication Problems, July 1978, 24 pp.). Because he so completely summmarized the Third World position, Masmoudi's argument is presented here at length.
4. "Television Traffic—A One Way Street?" UNESCO Reports and Papers on Mass Communication, no. 70 (1974), p. 44.
5. Herbert I. Schiller, "The Electronic Invaders," *The Progressive,* August 1973, pp. 23–25.
6. Schiller, "Madison Avenue Imperialism," *Trans-Action,* March-April 1971, p. 53.
7. Masmoudi, "New World Information," p. 22.
8. "Shadows over the Free Press," editorial in the *Milwaukee Journal,* July 19, 1976, p. 10.

8

Moving Together
or Further Apart?

THE World is moving in two directions: one is
towards the narrowing of distances through
travel, increasing interchange between scientists (who take a world view of problems such
as the exploration of space, ecology, population); the other is towards the shutting down
of frontiers, the ever more jealous surveillance
by governments and police of individual freedom.

—STEPHEN SPENDER
(poet and critic)

THE Planet Earth is clearly in trouble.

That was the conclusion of a 776-page U.S. government
study that warned: "If the present trends continue, the world in
2000 will be more crowded, more polluted, less stable ecologi-
cally, and more vulnerable to disruption than the world we live in
now."[1]

Prepared by 13 governmental agencies, the 1980 report
(three years in the making) to President Carter projected the
following trends:

• Rapid growth in world population—at a rate of 100 million
annually—will continue until the year 2000. The world's population, 4 billion in 1975, will be 6.35 billion at the end of the century, 90 percent of that growth coming in the poorest countries.

• The gap between the rich and poor nations will widen. Some of the less developed countries will raise their comparative income, but in the great populous regions of South Asia, income will remain below $200 a year.

• Arable land will increase only 4 percent by 2000, while population (as of 1975) will increase 50 percent. This could mean hunger for millions, with possible social unrest.

• World oil production will approach its limits. Many less developed countries will have difficulty meeting energy needs.

• Water supplies will become increasingly erratic as population growth doubles demand and the world's forests disappear at the rate of an area half the size of California each year, making water storage more difficult.

• Faulty land-use methods will turn global grassland into barren wasteland at a yearly rate equal to about the square mileage of the state of Maine.

The somber forecast concluded that only international cooperation can arrest the degradation of the world environment, resource exhaustion, and overpopulation. As we have shown, any such international cooperation to deal with the shared global dangers requires an effective, pervasive, and unfettered system of international news communication.

The expanded capacity to communicate news and information about a world that is becoming ever more interdependent in some small measure has begun to erase differences and improve understanding among diverse societies and peoples.

The better educated and more affluent in most nations know more about the outside world and have access to more information than ever before. The educated elites of the recently independent nations, small though they are in number, travel more and are more conversant with world affairs than their predecessors under colonialism.

The international news system, despite its inadequacies, moves a great deal more information at much faster speeds than ever before. Enhanced by color television pictures transmitted by communication satellites, a major news event abroad frequently has immense and dramatic impact. But words and pictures do not always bring understanding; in fact, just the opposite often results in so heterogeneous a world. The West's version of world news, collected and disseminated mainly by American and European journalists, often antagonizes peoples elsewhere, despite their dependence on these sources.

Reasons for Discontent

As the previous chapter indicates, many in the Third World seriously question the whole structure of international news communication and would replace it with a New World Information Order, which would reorder and significantly alter present methods of exchanging international news. Mustapha Masmoudi's indictment of the Western news media has been answered by others,[2] but it is important here to understand the place the media debate occupies on the world's developmental agenda. The Third World's frustration and antagonism toward Western communication media cannot be separated from the economic disparities between rich and poor nations, many of the latter having recently been colonies.

In Africa and elsewhere, the early 1960s was a time of political independence when newly established nations began what Julius Nyerere of Tanzania called the "terrible ascent to modernization." In all but a handful of nations, that ascent has not moved beyond the first rung. Political incompetence and instability, economic stagnation, and lack of growth characterize many new nations. In 1970, at the end of the heralded UN Development Decade, the poverty gap had widened, and dependence on the West for technology, financing, and trade had increased. Then, in 1974, came a call for a New International Economic Order, which was in essence a demand for a fairer share of the world's resources. If the industrialized West was indeed exploiting the poorer nations, as charged, then it followed that the mass media of the West must be playing a role in that domination. Rosemary Righter makes the point that the new nations turned their attention to communication only at the Fourth Non-Aligned Summit at Algiers in 1973 in the context of a program for economic cooperation. The national media, they agreed, must be strengthened as part of efforts to "eliminate the harmful consequences of the colonial era." From the outset, the attack on the information structure has been explicitly associated with the call for a new economic order.[3]

Not unexpectedly, soon afterward came a call for a New World Information Order to restructure a media system whose reporting was widely held to be responsible for the West's failure to respond to the trade, aid, and financial needs of the developing world.

In fact, the rich and poor nations have been debating at least since the late 1950s over how to redistribute the world's wealth in much the same way that media specialists have argued more recently over the free flow of information. There is no doubting the seriousness of the global economic disparities; an international commission headed by Willy Brandt issued a report in early 1980 calling for a comprehensive reordering of international priorities and a massive transfer of wealth to the Third World—not from reasons of charity but from the urgent necessity to head off world economic collapse in the 1980s or 1990s.[4]

To deal with such formidable problems, some Third World leaders see the need to restructure the international communication system so that it can assist with these pressing tasks and help achieve social justice—a clear invocation of the Developmental concept of the press. But under the Western concept, the press exists to acquire and maintain liberty. Liberty is not the same as social justice, and historical evidence unmistakably shows that when press freedom is sacrificed for some social goal, then political liberty and civil rights usually disappear.

To the Western journalist, the press must be independent of government, not an instrument of authority, so that it can report and expose the abuses of authority at home or abroad. Now more than ever, governments need watching and scrutiny. For whether democratic or despotic, only governments have the power to conscript soldiers and send them off on dubious foreign adventures, establish gulags, punish dissidents. Political regimes everywhere today, but especially in the Third World, have been marred by incompetence, corruption, and venality. Masmoudi's charges notwithstanding, some journalists believe that the Western press has done far too little critical reporting about the failures and abuses of political leadership throughout the world. This basic impasse over the proper purpose of international news communication and the relations between the press and government will continue and show few signs of alleviation.

Growing Further Apart

In addition to these basic philosophical differences, the onrush of rapid technological change is further widening the communications gap between rich and poor nations. Lacking skilled manpower and an industrial base and without a highly literate and affluent population, the poor nations are unable to participate fully in the new technetronic age. When most of a country's population live as illiterate peasants supported by subsistence agriculture, as is the case in much of Africa, Asia, and parts of Latin America, terms like "transnational data flow," "free flow of information," or even a "new world information order" have little practical meaning. For the communication revolution is being brought about by education and communication—both severely underdeveloped in Third World countries, even those rich in oil assets. As a result, the Third World to date is a victim, rather than beneficiary, of the technetronic revolution.

As one scholar said:

Whether the less developed countries grow rapidly or slowly, or not at all, almost inevitably many of them will continue to be dominated by intensifying feelings of psychological deprivation. In a world electronically intermeshed, absolute or relative underdevelopment will be intolerable, especially as the more advanced countries begin to move beyond that industrial era into which the less developed countries have as yet to enter. It is thus no longer a matter of the revolution of rising expectations. The Third World today confronts the specter of insatiable aspirations.[5]

There is a danger that the Third World will increasingly follow leaders who advocate noncooperation with industrial nations. The recent rise of radical Arab nationalism in southwest Asia is a case in point. And some interpret the proposals for a New World Information Order as a reactionary withdrawal from communication interdependency. Such a posture can only further isolate poor nations and ensure a widening chasm between them and the rich.

Recent developments in communication satellites show that

applications of the new technology are racing ahead in northern nations. Canada has been a pioneer in satellites of many types, and its ANIK series of comsats have demonstrated the new trend toward more powerful spacecraft and smaller ground stations.

In the United States, the use of satellites to deliver television programs to cable systems was an important development of the late 1970s. The combination of satellites, ground stations, and cable has been called the reinvention of television. Not only does it enlarge the scope of television with a multitude of new channels, low cost, and nationwide program distribution, it also transforms the medium itself; television is on the verge of offering a variety of special-interest programming plus a variety of nonvideo services.[6]

Other industrialized nations—Japan, Australia, Germany, Great Britain, France—are moving rapidly into satellite communication technology. But aside from the Arabsat television satellite planned for the Arab states, with an expected launch in 1982, little is happening in the Third World. Yet it is these nations—those least able to utilize these dramatic changes of the technetronic revolution—that could gain most from improvements in telecommunications. Such increasing disparities can only add to the frustrations and resentments of societies lacking in communications capability.

Friction between Western Nations

The combination of computers and telecommunications has greatly expanded the flow of all kinds of information, not merely news, between the highly industrialized Western nations, and this in turn has created strains and in some cases legal barriers to the information flow.

When a fire alarm sounds in Malmo, Sweden, a fireman types the address of the fire into a computer terminal and in less than a minute gets back a description of potential hazards at the scene. The computer that supplies this information is in Cleveland, Ohio. Distance is no longer a factor in long-distance communication, so a Cleveland computer company was able to submit the lowest bid for the contract.

Such high-speed transnational data flow is on the increase,

and various methods to slow or block it are part of an expanding "information war." Long frustrated by the U.S. lead in computer and communication fields, Europe has turned to a new form of protectionism. French minister of justice Louis Joinet voiced European concerns: "Information is power, and economic information is economic power. Information has an economic value, and the ability to store and process certain kinds of data may well give one country political and technological advantage over other countries. This, in turn, may lead to a loss of national sovereignty through supranational data flows."[7]

To protect their national sovereignty against this perceived threat, many European nations are enacting various data protection laws, mainly in the name of individual rights. For example, a number of European nations, including Sweden, France, and West Germany, have adopted laws on privacy that restrict the flow across national borders of computerized information about individuals. However, the argument could be made that such laws are designed primarily to protect economic interests, especially infant computer industries, against imports.

According to the Commerce Department, U.S. exports of communication goods and services tripled from 1960 to 1973 and totaled more than $1 billion a year in 1978. Computerized data networks have transformed airline reservations and international banking operations, and more than 100 West European businesses were operating private data networks across borders. Another study found that 190 American concerns, many linked by private data networks, were transacting significant amounts of business around the world. This included IBM, with 123,000 non-American employees in 117 countries.

Also included among the 190 U.S. firms, of course, were the Associated Press and United Press International, since international news gathering is very much a part of this phenomenon, and the agencies, naturally, are concerned about potential barriers to international data flow.

What Can Be Done?

Improvements in methods of collecting and distributing international news must come from several quarters. Journalists and mass communicators of the communications-rich Western nations can take a number of steps to improve their own effectiveness. Governments and journalists of the communications-poor, non-Western nations can do more to involve themselves in transnational news flow, both as senders and receivers. (Media in Africa, Asia, or South America carry very little news from other Third World countries or continents, even when it is available.) Finally, much can be accomplished by nations and journalists working together through international organizations to arrive at some consensus on policy questions and proposals for action.

Western Initiatives

Western media should gather and report more news of the developing world and do it with more understanding and regard for the problems and views of other nations. The coups, the economic disasters, the corruption, and the civil wars must be reported, of course. But the press also must provide more comprehensive, sustained reporting of foreign regions along with some historical perspective. The public requires more general knowledge of foreign politics so that, say, when Afghanistan suddenly dominates the news, it can react more knowledgeably. The West itself would benefit greatly from a better balanced flow of news.

Television news, still locked into a half-hour format, needs to expand its coverage and, furthermore, do more than provide blanket coverage of a single big story such as the hostages in Iran while virtually ignoring other important stories breaking, for example, in Rhodesia (now Zimbabwe), Lebanon, Western Sahara, or Central America. Western media should invest more money and human resources in the coverage of foreign news and not leave the immense task to the few organizations that send a handful of journalists abroad. And the newspapers and broadcast stations that do not maintain correspondents abroad should do a better job of using and editing the considerable amount of information now available from news services and syndicates.

Foreign editors and correspondents could make much more use, as well, of academic sources. Throughout American universities are hundreds of area specialists who have current and reliable information about every corner of the world. A political science professor, for example, who has just returned from a summer in Rwanda, could write an informative background story about a country rarely visited by foreign correspondents.

Western journalists could expand programs to train and encourage journalists from the Third World. Over the years, Western news agencies have helped establish national news agencies and prepared the personnel to run them; furthermore, a steady stream of newsmen and women have come to Western Europe and America for training and internships. Although Third World critics rarely acknowledge this assistance, it has been significant and could be enlarged.

Western media organizations should also consider selectively establishing newspapers in Third World nations. Although such a course would be frought with political risks and accusations of neocolonialist intrusion, similar previous ventures have been successful and have markedly influenced the level of journalism in the countries involved. Two of the best newspapers in black Africa today, the *Daily Times* of Nigeria and the *Daily Nation* of Kenya, were started and sustained by foreign capital and expertise. India has a number of vigorous and independent newspapers today because the British established good newspapers there in colonial days. After independence, they were completely taken over by Indians and serve that nation well.

Closer Western ties can be established between journalists of different nations through international professional organizations such as the International Press Institute, International Federation of Journalists, Inter American Press Association. This can only lead to better understanding of common problems and increased cooperation.

One recent organizational response by Western journalists to the Third World challenge was the formation in 1976 of the World Press Freedom Committee, supported by private media and operating independently of all governmental agencies. Besides encouraging increased interaction of Third World journalists with their counterparts in the United States, Western Europe, and developed nations of Latin America, the group is working to create a personnel pool to assist in developing countries, provide equipment donated by Western media, and establish an information clearinghouse on exchange, scholarships, internships, and technical journalism training programs. The committee in its first years dispersed over $50,000 in grants, raised from nongovernmental sources, including $20,000 to the University of Nairobi's School of Journalism.

In addition, the organization, comprising 34 journalistic affiliates on five continents, is also lobbying for reduction of the rates for transmitting news by telex, telephone, radio, or television to developing nations.

Finally, the Western news media must do a better job of explaining the importance of a free and unrestricted flow of news throughout the world. Many editors are themselves unaware of the challenge to the Western concept of journalism.[8]

Third World Initiatives

To better balance the flow of information, the news media in the nonindustrialized nations must be improved and expanded. This is clearly necessary, but it will not be easy because a nation's mass media grow only about as fast as its economic and social institutions. Although training and technological assistance from the West and from Socialist nations is important, the impetus for improvement and growth must come from within. Masmoudi's indictment of Western news gathering is a tacit admission that Third World media themselves are inadequate for the task of gathering and distributing global news. A few Western news agencies and other media should not enjoy a near monopoly on global news gathering, but they are certainly incapable of correcting the inadequacies of the world news system—nor should they be expected to.

How soon and how effectively the Third World can improve its news media may well depend on how the governments of its nations respond to these policy questions:

1. Will Third World nations cooperate in developing regional and continental telecommunications systems?

In Africa, for example, the new technology of long-distance communications can have a revolutionary potential for the sub-

Sahara by providing a truly continental system of telecommunications where none has existed before. An integrated complex of regional satellites, cable systems, ground stations, microwave relays, and improved FM and AM radio broadcasting can have important implications for intra-African exchanges of news, educational programs, television programming, high-speed data transfers, and telephones. Telephone service improved measurably after INTELSAT directly connected the capitals of most nations. The long-talked-about Pan African News Agency, in planning since 1963, could become a viable supplement to Western agencies if communications were improved. Still, such a system requires a degree of political stability and a spirit of cooperation that are still lacking.

2. Will Third World nations show more concern both for their own peoples' right to know and for an unimpeded exchange of information throughout the world?

Too much of the international news controversy has involved the claims of professional journalists versus the rights of governments to regulate news and information. In today's world, any person, whether born in Pakistan, Norway, Peru, or Tanzania, has the right, at least in theory, to acquire information that affects his or her own personal welfare and future. And the government under which that person lives should respect that right. A hopeless ideal, some will say, since the overwhelming majority of humankind live under authoritarianism and are far removed from mass communication. Nevertheless, that is the direction in which the world must move if it is to survive.

To have access to and participate in the global news system requires that information, news, technical data, and cultural fare be permitted to move unimpeded across borders. But the resentment, if not hostility, of some leaders to the "cultural intrusion" of the mass culture imported from the West has led to controls on the influx of such materials from abroad.

3. Will Third World nations encourage more diversity in news and information?

Regional news agencies and exchanges of news can be helpful and should be actively fostered, despite the real problems involved. A key question is whether Third World governments will provide their own journalists and broadcasters a greater degree of autonomy and independence. Journalism flourishes best in an atmosphere of freedom from government and corporate interference, but few journalists in non-Western nations are provided much latitude. Too many, unfortunately, work for dictatorial governments or are at the mercy of arbitrary political interference. Too few governments in the world today permit their own journalists the freedom to probe serious internal problems, much less allow them to criticize even mildly the performance of those in authority.

The challenge to the communications-poor nations is a strong one indeed. Professor and journalist Elie Abel of Stanford made the case very well:

It is putting the cart before the horse to speak of a truly worldwide communication system in the absence of concrete and costly steps at the national level to build the necessary infrastructure and to train the people who must operate it. That goal cannot be attained by a dozen more UN resolutions or UNESCO declarations. It will take massive investments and a new set of priorities on the part of individual developing nations. . . . Even if generous assistance is forthcoming, however, the main efforts will have to be made by the developing countries themselves. Only a country with a strong domestic communication system can expect to make its voice heard, and its weight felt, around the world.

The long term goal, call it a New Information Order if you like, will not be advanced by censorship, closed frontiers and internal monopolies on the flow of information, incoming as well as outgoing. All of these practices are, unfortunately, still rampant in many developing countries.[9]

Cooperation between Nations

As Abel's comments show, the debate over international news flow goes on and shows no real signs of abatement, much less resolution. The confrontation is most apparent during the meetings of international organizations such as the UN bodies (including the United Nations Educational, Scientific and Cultural Organization) and the 1979 World Administrative Radio Conference (WARC) and at conventions of academic organizations such as the International Communication Association.

These confrontations have been notable for the great amounts of rhetoric supported by minuscule amounts of research data. This is similar to what Phil Foisie of the *Washington Post* said about foreign news in general: "Too much opinion chasing too few facts."

Yet international organizations serve an extremely important function by providing a setting in which East and West, North and South, can somehow find ways to at least partially reconcile their differences. An important plateau was reached at Paris in November 1978 when the 146 member nations of UNESCO gave unanimous endorsement to a compromise declaration on world news coverage. The declaration, most of it couched in very general language, eliminated all mention of government control of the news and strongly endorsed the principle of a free flow of information, terming freedom of information a basic human right. But it also asserted the need for improving equilibrium in the flow of news between developing and developed countries and called for improvement of the Third World's news organization with help from industrialized countries.

The declaration was not binding on any country. However, Western advocates of a free press had feared that a draft condoning government control of the press would have given more support and encouragement to countries wishing to impose restrictions on press coverage.

The key votes in altering the original draft of the declaration, which endorsed state control, came from Third World countries, many of which are critical of Western news agencies. It was Western pledges of financial aid and training that swung Third World support to the compromise wording. Unfortunately, however, the United States has been quite slow to carry out its promises of training and aid for the poorer nations. This can only lead to further hostility at future UNESCO meetings.

A major contribution toward reconciliation of differences was made by UNESCO's International Commission for the Study of Communication Problems. Chaired by Sean MacBride, a Nobel Peace Prize laureate, the 16-member commission met for two years and issued its final report in February 1980. The report recommended that journalists have free access to all news sources, both official and unofficial, and that all censorship be abolished. The document also included a Soviet dissent that termed censorship a national, not international, issue that should be handled by individual countries as each saw fit.

While supporting journalists' rights of access to news, the study supported Third World concerns about the "colonial domination" of news distribution.

The MacBride commission also had some harsh words for private enterprise media ownership. "Special attention should be devoted to obstacles and restrictions which derive from the concentration of ownership, public or private, from commercial influences on the press and broadcasting, or from private or governmental advertising. The problem of financial conditions under which the media operate should be critically reviewed, and measures elaborated to strengthen editorial independence."[10]

The study also dealt with some concrete, nonideological concerns such as the importance of finding ways to reduce telecommunication and air mail rates for the dissemination of news. In addition, the report called for an international research and development effort to increase the supply of paper and newsprint in the world.

Some concepts developed during the two years of work were dropped or diluted. The idea of special status and protection for journalists was dropped because, the commission stated, it could lead to the licensing of reporters. An international code of ethics, strongly endorsed during the commission's deliberations, was held over "for further study," as was the right of reply to inaccurate reports.[11]

The MacBride Commission has not resolved all the issues, of course, and has in fact been criticized by those on both sides of the controversy. Indeed, the report implies only agreement that the controversy will continue. Global communications are in ferment, and during the 1980s, at least 19 major international conferences will be held relating to how the electromagnetic spectrum, the building blocks of communication, are to be allocated among all nations. Binding decisions will be made that can have profound effects on how international news and information move around the world.

At this time, it is impossible to predict whether the continuing controversy will lead to an improvement or a deterioration in the international news system. That system is intimately tied with and affected by the world's pressing problems—problems that require vigorous news media to publicize and explain before understanding and resolution can be achieved.

We are only at the threshold of efforts that must be made in the years ahead to identify and comprehend the nature of the various planes and surfaces of the prism that is our news gathering and distribution system. Only then can the beams of news refracting through it illuminate paths to understanding and accommodation which before have been roads to conflict and discord.

Notes

1. "Planet Earth in Trouble, Concludes U.S. Report," *Wisconsin State Journal,* July 25, 1980, p. 16.
2. See the responses provided by Rosemary Righter in *Whose News? Politics, the Press and the Third World* (New York: Times Books, 1978) and the essays by Leonard Sussman and Barry Rubin in *International News: Freedom Under Attack,* ed. Dante Fascell (Beverly Hills, Calif: Sage Publications, 1979).
3. Rosemary Righter, "What Reply to the Third World's Plea for Justice?" *IPI Report* 28 (September 1979): 9.
4. "Brandt Unveils His Plan," *Newsweek,* February 18, 1980, p. 63.
5. Zbigniew Brzezinski, *Between Two Ages: America's Role in the Technetronic Age* (New York: Viking Press, 1971), p. 35.
6. Les Brown, "From the Air: Programs by Satellite and Cable," *New York Times,* February 17, 1980, sec. 3, p. 1.
7. John Eger, "A War over Words," *Milwaukee Journal,* March 5, 1978, Sunday Forum, p. 1.
8. Professor Elie Abel of Stanford found that at a 1979 meeting of California newspaper publishers, only two persons out of a large group attending could identify the expression "New World Information Order."
9. I. William Hill, "U.S. Battles to Prevent Third World News Control," *Editor & Publisher,* August 4, 1979, p. 24.
10. I. William Hill, "Media Monopolies Hit in McBride Report," *Editor & Publisher,* February 2, 1980, p. 13.
11. "UNESCO Study Asks Press Rights; Soviet Stand on Censorship Cited," *New York Times,* February 23, 1980, p. 14.

SELECTED BIBLIOGRAPHY

ARLEN, MICHAEL J. *Living Room War.* New York: Viking Press, 1969.
_____. "The Air: The Eyes and Ears of the World." *The New Yorker,* January 6, 1975, pp. 52–56.
BAGDIKIAN, BEN. *The Information Machines.* New York: Harper & Row, 1971.
BLOCKER, JOEL. "The Bad News from UNESCO." *Columbia Journalism Review,* March/April 1976, pp. 57–59.
BROWN, LESTER R. *World without Borders.* New York: Vintage Books, 1973.
BRZEZINSKI, ZBIGNIEW. *Between Two Ages: America's Role in the Technetronic Era.* New York: Viking Press, 1971.
CHERRY, COLIN. *World Communication: Threat or Promise?* New York: Wiley Interscience, 1971.
CLARKE, ARTHUR C. "Beyond Babel: The Century of the Communications Satellite." In *The Process and Effects of Mass Communication,* ed. W. Schramm and D. Roberts, pp. 952–65. Urbana: University of Illinois Press, 1971.
Control of the Direct Broadcast Satellite: Values in Conflict. Palo Alto, Calif.: Aspen Institute Program on Communication, 1974.
DIZARD, WILSON P. *Television: A World View.* Syracuse, N.Y.: Syracuse University Press, 1966.
DUNCAN, CHARLES T. "The International Herald Tribune: Unique World Newspaper." *Journalism Quarterly* 50 (Summer 1973): 348–53.
EDELSTEIN, ALEX S.; BOWES, JOHN; AND HARSEL, SHELDON. *Information Societies: Comparing the Japanese and American Experiences.* Seattle: International Communication Center, School of Communications, University of Washington, 1978.

FASCELL, DANTE, ed. with essays by David Abshire, Leonard R. Suss-man, Barry Rubin, and Sean Kelly. *International News: Freedom under Attack.* Beverly Hills, Calif.: Sage Publications, 1979.

FISHER, GLEN. *American Communication in a Global Society.* Norwood, N.J.: Ablex, 1979.

FISCHER, HEINZ-DIETRICH, AND MERRILL, JOHN C., eds. *International Communication: Media, Channels, Functions.* New York: Hastings House, 1970.

GERBNER, GEORGE; GROSS, LARRY P.; AND MELODY, WILLIAM H., eds. *Communications Technology and Social Policy: Understanding the New "Cultural Revolution."* New York: John Wiley & Sons, 1973.

GOLDSBOROUGH, JAMES O. "An American in Paris—International Herald Tribune." *Columbia Journalism Review,* July/August 1974, pp. 37–45.

GREEN, TIMOTHY. *The Universal Eye.* London: Bodley Head, 1972.

GUBACK, THOMAS H. "Film as International Business." *Journal of Communication* 24 (Winter 1974): 90–101.

HACHTEN, WILLIAM A. "Ghana's Press under the NRC: An Authoritarian Model for Africa." *Journalism Quarterly* 52 (Autumn 1975): 458–64.

_____. *Muffled Drums: The News Media in Africa.* Ames: Iowa State University Press, 1971.

HEAD, SYDNEY, ed. *Broadcasting in Africa: A Continental Survey of Radio and Television.* Philadelphia: Temple University Press, 1974.

HESTER, ALBERT. "An Analysis of News Flow from Developed and Developing Nations." *Gazette* 17, no. 1, 2 (1974): 29–43.

_____. "International News Agencies." In *Mass Communication: A World View,* ed. Alan Wells, pp. 207–26. Palo Alto, Calif.: National Press Books, 1974.

HORTON, PHILIP C., ed. *The Third World and Press Freedom.* New York: Praeger, 1978.

HULTEN, OLOF. "The Intelsat System: Some Notes on Television Utilization of Satellite Technology." *Gazette* 19, no. 1 (1973): 29–37.

HUTH, DON. "World Services by Satellite, Landline or Bicycle." *The AP World* 28 (Summer 1971): 12.

KATZ, ELIHU. "News from the Global Village." *The Listener* 89 (January 18, 1973): 68–69.

KELLY, SEAN. *Access Denied: The Politics of Press Censorship.* Georgetown: Washington Papers, no. 55, 1978.

KLIESCH, RALPH. "A Vanishing Species: The American Newsman Abroad." New York: *Overseas Press Club Directory, 1975,* p. 18.

KOPKIND, ANDREW. "Publish and Perish." *More* 8 (April 1978): 13–16.

LASSWELL, HAROLD D. "The Future of World Communication: Quality and Style of Life." Papers of the East-West Communication Institute, Honolulu, no. 4, 1972.

LERNER, DANIEL. "Notes on Communication and the Nation State." *Public Opinion Quarterly* 37, no. 4 (Winter 1973–74): 541–50.

McGHEE, GEORGE C. "English—Best Hope for a World Language." *Saturday Review-World* 2 (November 30, 1974): 6, 57.

MADDOX, BRENDA. *Beyond Babel: New Directions in Communications.* Boston: Beacon Press, 1972.

MAISEL, RICHARD. "The Decline of Mass Media." *Public Opinion Quarterly* 37 (Summer 1973): 159–71.

MARKEL, LESTER, AND MARCH, AUDREY. *Global Challenge to the United States.* Cranbury, N.J.: Associated University Presses, 1976.

MASMOUDI, MUSTAPHA. *The New World Information Order.* Paris: UNESCO International Commission for the Study of Communication Problems, 1978.

MEISLER, STANLEY. "Covering the Third World (or trying to)." *Columbia Journalism Review,* November/December 1978, pp. 34–38.

MICKELSON, SIG. "Communication by Satellite." *Foreign Affairs* 48 (October 1969): 67–79.

MORRIS, ROGER. "Through the Looking Glass in Chile: Coverage of Allende's Regime." *Columbia Journalism Review,* November/December 1974, pp. 15–26.

MOWLANA, HAMID. "Who Covers America?" *Journal of Communication* 25 (Summer 1975): 86–91.

NORDENSTRENG, KAARLE, AND SCHILLER, HERBERT, eds. *National Sovereignty and International Communication.* Norwood, N.J.: Ablex, 1979.

NORDENSTRENG, KAARLE, AND VARIS, TAPIO. *Television Traffic—A One Way Street?* Paris: UNESCO Reports and Papers on Mass Communication, no. 70, 1974.

PELTON, JOSEPH N. *Global Communications Satellite Policy: Intelsat, Politics and Functionalism.* Mt. Airy, Md.: Lomond Books, 1974.

POOL, ITHIEL DE SOLA. "Communication in Communist Societies." In *Handbook of Communications,* ed. Wilbur Schramm, pp. 462–511. Chicago: Rand McNally, 1973.

_____. "Direct Broadcast Satellites and the Integrity of National Cultures." *Control of the Direct Broadcast Satellite: Values in Conflict.* Palo Alto, Calif.: Aspen Institute, 1974, pp. 27–35, 45–56.

PROSSER, MICHAEL H.,ed. *Intercommunication among Nations and Peoples.* New York: Harper & Row, 1973.

READ, WILLIAM. *America's Mass Media Merchants.* Baltimore: Johns Hopkins University Press, 1976.

_____. "International Newsweek vs. Newsweek." *Nieman Reports* 29 (Autumn, Winter 1975): 45–50.

_____. "Multinational Media." *Foreign Policy* 18 (Spring 1975): 155–67.

REISCHAUER, EDWIN O. *Toward the 21st Century: Education for a Changing World.* New York: Alfred A. Knopf, 1973.

RIGHTER, ROSEMARY. "What Reply to the Third World's Plea for Justice?" *IPI Report* 28 (September 1979): 9–12.

_____. *Whose News? Politics, the Press and the Third World.* New York: Times Books, 1978.

RIVERS, WILLIAM AND SCHRAMM, WILBUR. *Responsibility in Mass Communication.* New York: Harper & Row, 1969.

ROBINSON, GLEN O., ed. *Communications for Tomorrow: Policy Perspectives for the 1980s.* New York: Praeger, 1978.

ROSENBLUM, MORT. *Coups and Earthquakes: Reporting the World for America.* New York: Harper & Row, 1979.

_____. "Reporting from the Third World." *Foreign Affairs* 55 (July 1977).

RUBIN, BARRY. "International Censorship." *Columbia Journalism Review,* September/October 1975, pp. 55–58.

SCHAKNE, ROBERT. "Chile: Why We Missed the Story." *Columbia Journalism Review,* March/April 1976, pp. 60–62.

SCHILLER, HERBERT I. "Freedom from the 'Free Flow.'" *Journal of Communication* 24 (Winter 1974): 110–17.

_____. *Mass Communications and American Empire.* New York: Augustus Kelley, 1969.

_____. "The Electronic Invaders." *The Progressive,* August 1973, pp. 23–25.

_____. *The Mind Managers.* Boston: Beacon Press, 1973.

SHERMAN, CHARLES E. "The International Broadcasting Union: A Study in Practical Internationalism." *EBU Review* 25 (May 1974): 32–36.

SHERMAN, CHARLES E. AND RUBY, JOHN. "The Eurovision News Exchange." *Journalism Quarterly* 51 (Autumn 1974): 478–85.

SIEBERT, FRED; PETERSON, THEODORE; AND SCHRAMM, WILBUR. *Four Theories of the Press.* Urbana: University of Illinois Press, 1956.

STOKKE, OLAV, ed. *Reporting Africa.* New York: Africana Publishing, 1971.

SUSSMAN, LEONARD R. "A New World Information Order." *Freedom at Issue,* November/December 1978, pp. 4–10.

TUNSTALL, JEREMY. *The Media Are American: Anglo-American Media in the World.* London: Constable, 1977.

_____. "Worldwide News Agencies: Private Wholesalers of Public Information." Paper given at the Pacific Sociological Association meeting at Anaheim, Calif., April 1979.

20TH CENTURY FUND TASK FORCE ON THE FLOW OF NEWS. *A Free and Balanced Flow.* Lexington, Mass.: Heath, 1978.

UNESCO. *World Communications.* Paris: UNESCO Press, 1975.

VARIS, TAPIO. "Global Traffic in Television." *Journal of Communication* 24 (Winter 1974): 102–9.

WIGAND, ROLF T. "The Direct Satellite Connection: Definitions and Prospects." *Journal of Communication* 30, no. 2 (Spring 1980): 140–46.

WOOLLACOTT, MARTIN. "Western News-Gathering: Why the Third World Has Reacted." *Journalism Studies Review* 1, no. 1 (June 1976): 11–14.

INDEX